The Misteaching of Academic Discourses

The Politics of Language in the Classroom

Lilia I. Bartolomé

WestviewPress
A Division of HarperCollins*Publishers*

The Edge: Critical Studies in Educational Theory

Copyright © 1998 by Westview Press, A Division of HarperCollins Publishers, Inc.

Published in 1998 in the United States of America by Westview Press, 5500 Central Avenue, Boulder, Colorado 80301-2877, and in the United Kingdom by Westview Press, 12 Hid's Copse Road, Cumnor Hill, Oxford OX2 9JJ

Library of Congress Cataloging-in-Publication Data
Bartolomé, Lilia I.
    The misteaching of academic discourses : the politics of language
in the classroom / Lilia I. Bartolomé.
        p.   cm. — (The edge, critical studies in educational theory)
    Includes bibliographical references and index.
    ISBN 0-8133-3144-7 (hardcover)
    1. Communication in education—Social aspects—United States.
2. Socially handicapped children—Education—United States.
3. Language and education—Social aspects—United States.
4. Teaching—Social aspects—United States.   5. Critical pedagogy—
United States.   6. Multiculturalism—United States.   I. Title.
II. Series.
LB1033.5.B37   1998
370'.1'4—dc21
                                                                            98-9693
                                                                            CIP

The paper used in this publication meets the requirements of the American National Standard for Permanence of Paper for Printed Library Materials Z39.48-1984.

10   9   8   7   6   5   4   3   2   1

The Misteaching of
Academic Discourses

THE EDGE: CRITICAL STUDIES IN EDUCATIONAL THEORY

Series Editors   Joe L. Kincheloe, Peter McLaren, and Shirley Steinberg

---

To the two men in my life.

To my son, Alejandro Donaldo Macedo,
whose presence in the world gives me hope for a better tomorrow.

To my compañero, *Donaldo Macedo,*
whose mentorship, support, and cariño
made this book a reality.

Contents

Foreword

James Paul Gee

For quite some time now, we have asked: Why do so many minority and poor children fail in school? And, indeed, mounds of research devoted to this question have piled up, even as these children continue to fail. Lilia Bartolomé crucially changes the question. For her, the question is: How and why do we manage to fail to teach so many minority and poor children in school? The answers to this question are liable to make us all uncomfortable in ways that answers to the traditional question did not.

The answers to the traditional question—Why do so many minority and poor children fail at school?—often ran something like this: These children, like all of us, learn early in life how to use and understand language in the context of daily, face-to-face interaction with people with whom they share lots of experiences and information. Such "contextualized language" gets most of its meaning from the contexts in which it is used and the shared understandings on which it is based, not from the words uttered. However, many minority and poor children come to school unprepared for "school language." Such language, the language of lectures and books, is, it is held, "decontextualized." That is, such language is rendered meaningful not by the contexts in which it is used or on the basis of shared experiences but solely on the basis of what the words and sentences uttered or written literally mean. Such language is "explicit"; everyday, "contextualized language" is "inexplicit."

Bartolomé realizes that this account and, indeed, the whole notion of "decontextualized language" is misleading and harmful. All language is meaningful only in and through the contexts in which it is used. All language is meaningful only on the basis of shared experiences and shared information. All language is "inexplicit" until listeners and readers fill it out, based on the experiences they have had and the information they have gained in prior socioculturally significant interactions with others.

There is, in fact, no such thing as "school language" or "academic language" as a single entity. There are, rather, many different school languages and different styles of language used in different school practices. Similarly, there are many different academic languages and different styles of language used in different disciplines and different academic practices. There are, too, many different sorts of public-sphere language—different styles of language used for a variety of civic, economic, and political purposes. None of these many styles of language is "decontextualized." They are all—just like "everyday," face-to-face language—"contextualized."

But it is important here to see the word *contextualized* as naming an active process: the process of a person "contextualizing," that is, making and doing a context, not just passively registering one. What does it mean to say we humans actively "contextualize" language? "Context" is not just "out there." We do not just "reflect" context when we speak or write. Rather, we always actively create "context." We make the world around us mean certain things.

If I go up to a female colleague and in "everyday talk" say, "You look great this morning," this means little or nothing until that person has actively construed the context in a certain way. She may take the context to be "friendly banter between colleagues" or "intended or unintended sexual harassment" or "encouragement for someone who cares too much about her looks" or "joking with someone who cares little about her looks" or "irony meant to defuse a 'politically correct' environment" or whatever. She consults what she knows about me and herself, our mutual histories, where we are and what it means to be there here and now, and a myriad of other factors, in order to actively construe the context in a certain way. In fact, she can go so far as to respond in ways that make me, the speaker, reconstrue the context to be the way she wants it to be (for example, I realize that my remark would not have been made to a male and I see its sexual side). Or I can resist. Context is also something we negotiate, fight over, and sometimes smoothly and harmoniously share; thus, we forget how much work we are, in fact, doing to "pull off" context.

This "contextualizing work" is something we do in all cases of language. But how do we manage it? We can only make a context mean a certain thing if we have the resources to make it mean that. And what are those resources? They are simply this: having had experiences with others in construing contexts that way—in other words, interacting with others who, at least initially, know how to construe contexts that way better than we do. If the female teacher does not know how to construe the context of "you look great this morning" as "intended or unintended sexual harassment," then she just has not "hung out" long enough with the right sort of "feminists" or has not had (or empathized with) the sorts of experiences many women have had in the workplace. In this sense, learning to contextualize and contextualizing are always "social" and "cultural" phenomena. A way of contextualizing always belongs to some group or community of people with their own interests and practices, based on experiences they have had in the world.

One learns no variety of language without having fully and repeatedly participated in the typical experiences that render that form of language meaningful. All that I have said thus far is as true of any school-based, academic, specialist, or public-sphere variety of language as it is of everyday talk. To see this, consider a sentence I have taken at random from a "popular" book by a physicist (F. David Peat, *Einstein's Moon*, Contemporary Books, 1990, p. 146): "Bell's theorem has spelled the end to hidden mechanical variables and local ideas of reality." Remember, this is just the sort of language that is supposed to be "decontextualized," that is, understandable based on its words and sentence structure alone.

What does it take to understand this sentence (or the book it is in)? It takes having had the sorts of experiences that would allow one to construe a context or contexts in which this sentence would be meaningful. And what would those experiences have been? They would have been familiarity with certain texts, with certain issues and debates, with certain practices inside and outside laboratories, and with certain ways of talking and viewing the world. It is, by the way, very rare, indeed, that people understand this sort of language if all they have ever done is read books. Without having had the opportunity to engage in discussion with people who use this sort of language and without having experienced some of what such people do, where they do it, and why they do it, it is very hard, indeed, to gain real understanding—just as hard as it is to learn French only by reading French books.

Sometimes, instead of drawing the "contextualized"-"decontextualized" distinction, people draw a related distinction between language that is heavily "deictic" and language that is not. *Deictic* is a fancy word that means "pointing." Things such as pronouns and demonstratives are deictics because they "point" outside the utterances they are in to the larger context. For example, in a sentence such as "he's funny because he does things like that," *he* and *that* point to things outside the utterance itself. Everyday speech is full of such deictics that "tie" it tightly to its context.

But the sentence from the physics book is full of pointers of a different sort. "Bell's theorem" points to an earlier discussion of a particular piece of mathematical physics and thus, too, to one's previous experiences with both physics and mathematics. "Hidden mechanical variables" points via "variables" to one's previous experience with experimentation inside and outside physics. It points via "mechanical" to one's experiences with both machines and machine metaphors and the whole Western history of mechanistic explanations of nature. It points via "hidden" to one's previous experiences of explanations, inside and outside physics proper, that appeal to not easily observable or even invisible entities in order to offer a "causal" explanation of observable phenomena. "Local ideas of reality" points via "local" to a contrast between "local" and "nonlocal" and, thereby, to one's experiences of (nonlocal) "causes" that are far removed and seemingly unconnected to their "effects" (experiences few of us, in fact, have had, so this bit is hard even for people who have had enough experiences to imagine contexts for the other bits of the sentence). The moral is this: All language is heavily deictic, though different types of language point in different ways to different sorts of experiences.

I must admit that as a child growing up, I never had most of the sorts of experiences that would render language like that from the physics book (or juvenile versions of such language) meaningful. In fact, I was raised in a family and community that had no chance for such experiences. I arrived at college having had no opportunity whatsoever to develop the prerequisite understandings of and experiences in science and mathematics. But ironically, perhaps, my later forms of schooling were all based on the assumption that I must have had such opportunities, and thus, my failures to understand must therefore have been based on either ignorance or a lack of desire.

Someone might have asked, had anyone phrased the issue that way in those days, why "white trash" like me failed to be able to learn math and science. The answer would have been obvious to me even then, though at the time I had no interest in education: because "white trash" were never allowed to have the necessary experiences. We never got to "play" with the people, places, tools, or books that could have given us such experiences. But to have said this out loud would have raised issues of "class" and "fairness" and the distribution of "good schooling" in the United States, issues that were deeply taboo then and are not much less so today, despite the pretensions we academics adopt.

It is the scandal of U.S. society that the doors not just to physics but also to the most central sorts of "school-based" and public-sphere language—the sorts of language connected to power in our society and virtually taken by those in power as constituting intelligence and full humanity—do not exist for a great many children, either early in life or later. When these children fail in school, we ask why they have failed. We do not, then, have to ask who it was that failed them. To use a sports metaphor, for poor people and many minorities, it is as if the students get "cut slips" from a team for which they were never allowed to try out.

This situation—where we can attribute failure to the children rather than to our society, where people can get cut slips for teams they were never allowed to try out for—works because we systematically hide information on just what experiences and how many of them are necessary to develop the ability to construe and imagine contexts that render "specialist" forms of language truly and deeply meaningful. We pretend that it is easy to make up for a lack of these experiences late in the game, though no one thinks most of us could make the college basketball team if we had never played basketball previously. Some (lucky) people can do it (though they usually have to cover up their gaps), but it is a sin to make people feel they are failures when, late in the game, they do not "make the team" in competition with others who have played the game all their lives.

Lilia Bartolomé replaces the term *decontextualized language* with the term *linguistically contextualized language*, and it is important to be clear about what this really means. School-based, academic, specialist, and public-sphere forms of language are "linguistically contextualized" in the important sense that, in all cases, the child is learning a new (variety of) language, a language different from the language of the "lifeworld." They are "linguistically contextualized" as well, in the important sense that many of the experiences children must have to be able to contextualize this new variety of language are experiences with new types of texts and talk. In this sense, ideas about language acquisition and development are crucial to all school learning. But to understand a new specialist variety of language, children must learn to actively contextualize it in terms of the new experiences they are having in and out of school, not only with new types of text and talk but also with new ways of thinking, believing, knowing, feeling, acting, and interacting with other people and various sorts of places, objects, tools, and technologies.

There is some sense to the notion of "decontextualized language" but not the sense most people who use the term intend. School-based, specialist, academic, and public-sphere languages, though always requiring acts of active contextualizing, are decontextualized from people's lifeworlds. By *lifeworlds*, I mean the culturally distinctive (different cultures have different lifeworlds) ways of being, acting as, and talking as an "everyday," nonspecialist person. School-based, specialist, academic, and public-sphere forms of language often require us to exit our lifeworlds and construe contexts based on experiences we have had outside these lifeworlds—experiences in classrooms, laboratories, concert halls, academic discussions, research projects, civic institutions, businesses, and so forth.

When we exit our lifeworlds, the worlds we all live in when we are being "everyday people" and not speaking out of some specialist domain or another, we leave "home," in a sense. For many advantaged children, this trip is not really very treacherous. They are not asked to deny and denigrate their lifeworlds in the process. In fact, from the outset, their induction into specialist domains has been facilitated via rich bridges to their lifeworlds. Their lifeworlds have, in fact, incorporated, from early on, some of the practices and values of specialist domains, though, of course, in attenuated forms (for example, early reading of "children's literature," a bridge to the specialist domain of "literature" proper). For many minority and poor children, by contrast, no such bridges exist or are built. We rarely build on their experiences and on their very real, distinctive lifeworld knowledge. In fact, these children are often asked, in the process of being exposed to specialist domains, to deny the value of their lifeworlds and their communities in reference to those of more advantaged children.

Bartolomé knows all this. She is well aware, too, that the only real solution is to change the game, that is, to change our society. The only real solution is to imagine and begin to implement a society in which success in school and having access to specialized forms of knowledge are not markers of class and race and, in some cases, gender. But she is also aware that we can do much better in school while we are waiting for the "revolution."

First, we can tell the truth, as Bartolomé is telling it—the truth about the distribution of experiences in our society. We can be honest with people about where they have entered the game and how much work it is going to take to "catch up." We can be honest with people about the fact that catching up may not always be possible (after all, the elites do not just stop having experiences), so that other strategies may be necessary, as well. We can be honest, too, about the fact that minority and poor children need not just better schools than they currently have but also better schools even than the schools we typically give to the elites, who, after all, have experiences outside school that compensate for what are often, in truth, mediocre schools (despite the price of the houses in their neighborhoods).

Bartolomé begins to suggest what those better schools might look like. Let me end by suggesting a "bill of rights" for all children but most especially for minority and poor children. This bill of rights would be based partly on the work of the Multiliteracies Project (see "A Pedagogy of Multiliteracies: Designing Social Futures," *Harvard Educational Review* 66(1996):60–92) and partly on inspiration I have drawn from Lilia Bartolomé's book. Every child—but most especially those children who have heretofore been excluded from the experiences that would allow them to contextualize school-based, specialist, academic, and public-sphere forms of language—has a moral right to four forms of integrated instruction:

1. They have a right to lots of situated practice. By "situated practice," I mean "hands-on," embodied experiences of authentic and meaningful social practices (involving talk, texts, tools, and technologies) of the sort that help one imagine contexts that render what is being taught meaningful. If children are learning science, they have a right to see, feel, hear, and practice meaningful and authentic science with all its linguistic, technological, cognitive, and social accoutrements (I have seen second-graders doing this). And they have a right to have this sort of situated practice in a way that, far from denigrating their lifeworlds, makes bridges to them.

2. They have a right to overt instruction. By "overt instruction," I mean all forms of guidance and scaffolding, within and outside situated practice, that focus the learner's attention, in a reflective and meta-aware way, on the important parts of the language and practice being taught. Overt instruction, in this sense, foregrounds the (cognitively, socially, and historically) important patterns and relationships in the language and practices being taught. For example, Western physics makes an important distinction between "underlying realities" and "superficial appearances." Children learning physics have a right to be made overtly aware that this is important, to know why it is important, and to know what sorts of language and practices follow from its importance.

3. They have a right to critical framing. By "critical framing," I mean ways of coming to know where in the overall system the student stands. How does what he or she is learning relate to other domains? Where in the overall system of knowledge and social relations does the language and knowledge he or she is learning stand? For instance, the distinction physicists make between "underlying realities" (for example, fundamental particles) and "superficial appearances" (for example, the solidity of objects) has been imported to many other domains, and in some of these it has been used for pernicious purposes (such as underlying racial characteristics, genetic determinism, or a single underlying mental variable called "intelligence").

4. They have a right to be allowed to produce and transform knowledge, not just consume it. Children should, indeed, master the standard "genres" of many school-based, specialist, academic, and public-sphere forms of language and social practices, but they should also know how to transform them, break them, and innovate new ones for their own social, cultural, and political purposes. In fact, they should know that even in using the standard genres, they are (or should be) always actively adapting them to their own purposes, customizing them to the contexts they as actors are trying to create.

Ultimately, our failure of minority and poor children in school is rooted in our unwillingness or inability to give them the forms of instruction that are theirs by right and that are necessitated by the doors that have and continue to be closed to them. The advantages of advantaged children lie primarily in the experiences described in the first article of the bill of rights just presented, though ironically, these sorts of experiences are often provided by their families in out-of-school sites. The other forms of instruction can begin to help disadvantaged children "catch up" and, given the metaknowledge and political awareness implied by articles 3 and 4, move beyond those who have attempted to keep the game to themselves. Lilia Bartolomé's book is a courageous attempt to change how we think about minority and poor children and schools. It is a courageous attempt, as well, to begin to imagine a socially just society, a world in which no one's lifeworld is denigrated and in which all the worlds we humans create beyond the lifeworld are open to all.

1 *Understanding Academic Discourses*

The education of low-status linguistic-minority students in the United States can be generally characterized as a form of miseducation that continues to produce an unacceptably high rate of failure.[1] The miseducation of linguistic-minority students is particularly noticeable among Latinos in general and Mexican Americans in particular.[2] Although the majority of all students begin their schooling with more or less the same hopes, aspirations, and dreams, a high percentage of linguistic-minority students who enter high school never graduate, compared to 17 percent of Anglo students. Approximately 45 percent of Mexican American students drop out of school, and in some communities, the dropout rate is even higher. Because of the schools' failure to educate the largest Latino subgroup—Mexican Americans—and because of this subgroup's *historical, pervasive,* and *disproportionate* academic underachievement, it is particularly urgent to better understand the multiple variables that influence the poor academic performance of these students.[3] In addition to the intolerably high rate of academic failure, the projected increases for the Mexican American population dramatically illustrate the need for immediate academic intervention for these students as early as elementary school.[4] Given the complexity of this problem, the high dropout rate and the academic failure of Mexican Americans have directly and indirectly generated numerous research studies examining the underachievement phenomenon from a variety of perspectives.

From a linguistic perspective, which is the focus of this book, the academic failure of Mexican American students has historically been attributed to their lack of English-language proficiency.[5] However, recent research shows that proficiency in English, in and of itself is not sufficient for academic success. Although common perception suggests that the English proficiency of most Mexican American students is limited, a significant number of these students are bilingual in English and Spanish.[6] Nevertheless, many English-proficient bilingual Mexican American stu-

1

dents continue to experience difficulties and failure in school. In fact, studies suggest that U.S.-born, English-dominant Mexican-American students may actually experience more academic failure than their foreign-born, Spanish-dominant peers who have recently arrived in the United States; the latter may not have mastered English, but they are literate in their first language and have learned to communicate their knowledge via the academic discourses of their native language.[7]

The concept of "academic discourses" refers to more than just the student's ability to produce standard English by using the correct phonology (sound system), lexicon (vocabulary), and syntax (sentence structure). In addition to these three language dimensions, less easily measured language components such as cultural knowledge about rhetorical structures (the ability to create texts whose logic and structure reflect academic and mainstream ways of organizing texts) are equally important. For example, one valued academic discourse strategy involves the ability to produce texts that reflect a unidimensional and linear line of argument.

James Gee, Sarah Michaels, and other researchers have shown that working-class African American students often produce utterances in English that are difficult for their middle-class white teachers to understand.[8] The communication difference often lies in the manner in which the students organize their texts and utilize contextual cues. For example, Sarah Michaels reported that middle-class white teachers often evaluated the narratives their African American students offered during sharing time as unwieldy, illogical, and confusing;[9] this was because the children (1) produced oral text structures that did not follow a linear line of thought, (2) assumed the audience shared their background knowledge, and (3) utilized culturally specific intonation cues to signal emphasis.[10] (A more detailed discussion of this body of literature is presented in Chapter 2.)

In the case of Mexican American students, the research suggests that older, recently arrived students who received their previous education in Mexican schools often come to U.S. classrooms already possessing knowledge about academic rhetorical structures and communication practices that are valued in school contexts and necessary for success, particularly if they come from middle-class backgrounds.[11] These students may be temporarily handicapped because of their limited proficiency in English; however, once they acquire a threshold level of proficiency in English, they eventually are able to transfer their Spanish academic discourse skills to English, thus guaranteeing some degree of success in the classroom.

Ironically, Mexican American students born and bred in the United States often are not similarly skilled. This is because, unlike their Mexican peers, they usually have not had the opportunity to develop academic discourse skills in their primary language in a school context that supports their full linguistic development. The sad irony is that schools often require from these linguistic-minority students precisely those academic discourse skills and knowledge bases that they often do not teach. This is what Donaldo Macedo has called a "pedagogy of entrapment," in that teachers require of students what they do not explicitly teach them.[12] In other words, even well-intentioned teachers often fail to overtly teach the academic discourses necessary for school success.[13]

Even in bilingual education classrooms designed to help students with limited English proficiency make the transition into English-only classrooms, teachers often make false assumptions concerning the level of the linguistic-minority students' ability to use English academic discourses; moreover, they seldom teach these discourses explicitly to these students. Teachers often fail to understand that the academic discourses prerequisites are not inherently part of these students' working-class, native-language competency. For example, most of the Mexican American students I have worked with come from a working-class reality and speak a variety of Spanish different from the Spanish academic discourse generally taught in bilingual programs. Thus, they are often confronted with two major linguistic problems: a lack of proficiency in the academic discourse in their second language, English, and a similar lack in their native language, Spanish. Hence, to assume that these students will automatically transfer a presumed academic metalinguistic awareness in the first language to the second represents a form of entrapment. That is, teachers require these students to have linguistic competency in the academic discourse that they were never taught in *either* language. One unfortunate result is that many linguistic-minority students in either English-only or bilingual settings are not being explicitly prepared to comprehend and produce more formal academic speech and writing in any language.

The Myth of "De-Contextualized" Language

The very real pedagogical entrapment experienced by linguistic-minority and other working-class students contradicts much of the "common-sense" presumption that in school settings, teachers actually teach students more "academic" ways of communicating and students simply fail to acquire these more advanced communication skills. It is commonly accepted that an academic discourse that relies on linguistic cues such as precise vocabulary and unilaterally structured syntactic and rhetorical structures is more communicatively efficient in an academic setting. Unfortunately, the reality is that academic discourse conventions are seldom explicitly taught to working-class, linguistic-minority students.[14] Furthermore, there is also a tendency to glorify and romanticize a particular type of academic language discourse that is inaccurately referred to in the literature as "de-contextualized" language. I say "inaccurately" because language production for meaningful communication cannot be achieved outside the cultural context that gives the produced language meaning in the first place. In other words, all language is context bound in one manner or another.

A variety of terms have been used to identify so-called de-contextualized language. It has been referred to by researchers as *literate or autonomous language,*[15] *school language,*[16] *disembedded language,*[17] *less contextualized language,*[18] and *situation-independent language.*[19] These terms all attempt to capture the numerous language features related to a text's overt levels of precision, explicitness, and clarity. However, the use of these apparently innocuous and "objective" terms hides the reality that dominant ideology often devalues language varieties that do not conform to the prescribed rules of the standard academic discourse.

For instance, it is assumed that speakers of the standard academic discourse generate meaning outside of context, conveying explicit and precise messages that would be universally understood without relying on the specificity of context to access meaning. The assumption here is that the working-class dialect is context bound, whereas the standard academic discourse transcends social and cultural locations and is therefore more universal, less localized, and more autonomous. The very use of the term *dialect* to refer to the working-class language variety signals the devaluation of this variety and its speakers. By using the standard academic discourse as a yardstick against which all other varieties are measured, one begins to view nonstandard discourses negatively, for they "lack" the features attributed to the standard discourse (which is, coincidentally also, the dominant variety). This valuation process hides the asymmetrical power relationship between the dominant standard discourse and all other, nonstandard varieties. For example, rarely do we refer to the standard discourse as a dialect, even though, linguistically speaking, it is just that. The term of preference for the dominant standard discourse is usually *language.* Thus, middle- and upper-class students, particularly whites, speak a language whereas lower-class racial and ethnic groups speak a dialect, which, among other features, is characterized by its lack of autonomy from its social and cultural contexts.

Researchers who, in the name of science, create (or sustain) a false dichotomy between *de-contextualized* and *contextualized* discourse fail to realize that their coinage of these terms is false in that no discourse exists outside context; they also fail to realize that they play a key role in reproducing the dominant ideology, which is often hidden by the language they use to describe different linguistic varieties. The so-called de-contextualized discourse implies linguistic superiority while making its context invisible. How does one explain the fact that middle- and upper-class white students can answer questions on scholastic achievement tests (SATs) without having to actually read the accompanying passages? James Gee, for example, gave his students in an honors program (mostly populated by middle- and upper-class whites) at the University of Southern California the following SAT questions.[20]

1. The main idea of the passage is that
   A) a constricted view of [this novel] is natural and acceptable
   B) a novel should not depict a vanished society
   C) a good novel is an intellectual rather than an emotional experience
   D) many readers have seen only the comedy [in this novel]
   E) [this novel] should be read with sensitivity and an open mind

2. The author's attitude toward someone who enjoys [this novel] and then remarks "but of course it has no relevance today" (lines 21–22) can best be described as one of
   A) amusement
   B) astonishment
   C) disapproval
   D) resignation
   E) ambivalence

3. The author [of this passage] implies that a work of art is properly judged on the basis of its
   A) universality of human experience truthfully recorded
   B) popularity and critical acclaim in its own age
   C) openness to varied interpretations, including seemingly contradictory ones
   D) avoidance of political and social issues of minor importance
   E) continued popularity through different eras and with different societies

Nearly 100 students who answered these questions answered them correctly 80 percent of the time without reading the accompanying passages. In fact, Gee noted, "virtually no student has missed the answer to question 3 (which is A)."[21] However, when he gave the same questions to his "regular" undergraduate students (among whom there was more diversity along class, race, and ethnicity lines), "a great many more students answered them incorrectly."

What guided the students in the honors program to answer the questions correctly without reading the passages? Gee explained:

> Avant-garde literary critics certainly do not believe that a work of art is properly judged on the basis of its universality of human experience truthfully recorded. In fact, they believe something must closer to answer C; A work of art is properly judged on the basis of its openness to varied interpretations, including seemingly contradictory ones. And my honors students do not, in fact, believe that a work of art is properly judged on the basis of its universality of human experience truthfully recorded, either. They are prone to believe something much closer to answer E: A work of art is properly judged on the basis of continued popularity through different eras and with different societies.
>
> Why do my honors students answer A to question 3? They do so because they immediately recognize, in this question and the others, a certain set of values. They recognize a value like "truth and beauty transcend cultures," so they know that the answer to question 3 is A. They recognize a value like "truth and beauty transcend time," so they know that the answer to question 2 is C. And they recognize a value like "truth and beauty are open (and only open) to people who are appropriately sensitive and open minded" (that is, people who are not "ideological"), thus they know that the answer to question 1 is E.[22]

As this SAT test experiment exemplified, students socialized in a particular set of values that correspond to those values held by the dominant institutions (such as schools and testing centers) had no difficulty answering the test questions correctly even when they did not read the questions' accompanying passages. They did so because they were guided by a set of values required through their class and culture socialization rather than by any innate intelligence predisposition.

As Gee also correctly argued, these students even betrayed their own beliefs so as to adhere to what they believed was a dominant consensus— a set of values shared by the dominant sector of the society. I would point out that the set of values that guided these students to the correct answers without reading the questions represented a contextual point of reference for meaning-making similar to the visible, context-bound signposts used by working-class racial and ethnic students in their own meaning-making. The difference is that in the so-called de-contextualized discourse, the point of reference is often made invisible in keeping with the inner workings of ideology. What is at work in the nomenclature of "de-contextualized discourse" is how students "respond appropriately to a specific hegemonic or displaced consensus centered on the values of dominant Discourses, a consensus achieved among persons (in the dominant groups or not) whose paths through life have [for a time and place] fallen together with the members of these dominant Discourses."[23]

Hence, the teaching and acquisition of the dominant academic discourse requires much more than linguistic knowledge. It requires knowledge about "ways of being in the world, ways of acting, thinking, interacting, valuing, believing, speaking, and sometimes writing and reading, connected to particular identities and social roles."[24] If a teacher fails to acknowledge that certain groups of students who come from subordinated cultural and racial groups do not have access to and membership in the dominant discourse, he or she makes the power of the dominant discourse invisible and also reproduces the distinction (often invisible) that is inherent in the dominant discourse and that serves as a measure in society as a whole. Thus, teaching and the acquisition of the dominant discourse would inevitably involve democratizing social structures so that the dominant academic discourse and the social, economic, and political structures it sustains become more accessible to subordinated students. Despite the ideological nature of this type of discourse, the operationalization of so-called de-contextualized language in the literature has tended to focus on solely linguistic features that render written and oral text overtly explicit, such as using precise vocabulary and syntax.

Operationalizing "De-Contextualized" Language

Much of the current educational research identifies numerous linguistic features, all related to a text's overt levels of explicitness and implicitness, in its operationalization of "de-contextualized" language. Researchers' foci range from the use of lexical and prosodic cues to the complexity of sentence structure and the use of pronouns, as well as the texts' overall cohesiveness.

These researchers recognize that, in reality, so-called de-contextualized language is not truly *de*-contextualized (that is, devoid of all context) but rather is contextualized using chiefly linguistic cues and strategies restricted to the text to render a message explicit, instead of relying on extralinguistic cues or cues located outside the sentence (such as use of body language, varying intonation, and assumptions of shared knowledge with interlocutors). However, the researchers stop short of recognizing that these linguistic cues and strategies rely on values that become the contextual point of reference. (See Chapter 2 for a more fully developed review of the body of literature produced by these researchers.)

Nonetheless, linguists such as James Gee are quick to point out that all language is contextualized, and they remind us of the culture-specific nature of using and valuing language that is linguistically contextualized. In fact, Gee has specifically linked children's ability to speak in "school-like" ways with their socialization in "school-like" home cultures:

> Certain cultures, as well as unschooled people in our culture, simply do not have, and thus do not use, the conventions prevalent in our schools that in certain contrived situations (like "show and tell time") one pretends that people do not know or see what they obviously do know and see. . . . Such assumptions—that one should ignore what the hearer knows and explicitly say it anyway—are . . . the hallmark of many middle-class home-based practices with children (e.g., having the child repeat back an often read book or rehearse at the dinner table daily events that one already knows about). In other social groups . . . such explicitness may be seen as rude because it is distancing, blunt or condescending to the hearer's intelligence.[25]

As Gee suggested, certain cultural and social groups place great value on producing texts that are overtly explicit and do not require interlocutor negotiation. That is, more middle-class and schooled ways of contextualizing text require distance between interlocutors so that the only visible cues for making meaning are linguistic ones.

I use the more specific descriptor *linguistically contextualized*, rather than the more conventional *de-contextualized language*, because, as discussed, the latter term erroneously connotes that language can, indeed, be *de*-contextualized, that is, free of all context. The use of this popular term obfuscates the fact that *de-contextualized language* actually refers to language that utilizes the mainstream or dominant culture's preferred ways of contextualizing. I believe that the term *linguistically contextualized* constitutes a more accurate and objective descriptor of the type of language strategies we value in schools; it also does not perpetuate the erroneous and almost mystical air surrounding the term *de-contextualized language*.

For example, the use of text-organizing strategies such as the "topic-centered" organization of narratives that middle-class white children use (presenting a main point or theme and then elaborating about only that point or theme) and the use of specific linguistic cues (such as introductory sentences that inform the listener of the speaker's main point as well as his or her plans for organizing and presenting the text) are treated in the literature not as culturally specific ways of contextualizing oral and written messages but as text that is *de*-contextualized.[26] Described as *de*-contextualized text, it is thus believed to be capable of transmitting meaning on its own, irrespective of the context in which the communicative effort takes place.

Despite the *linguistic* reality that so-called *de*-contextualized language really is not free of all contextual information and cues, the *social* reality is that not all contextualizing conventions or strategies are perceived as equally valuable by the dominant culture. The use of linguistic cueing is perceived as more desirable and cognitively superior than relying on subordinate cultural cues (body language, the use of prosodic cues such as changing intonation, and so forth). Here, we begin to see how the dominant valuation system operates through distinction so as to asymmetrically distribute cultural goods. In fact, as argued earlier, even the so-called de-contextualized discourse relies on extralinguistic structures such as value systems to generate meaning. To a great extent, especially in classroom situations in which students manage to communicate their intent, these preferences for form over content reflect social and cultural preferences rather than purely linguistic value.

I believe that as educators committed to improving the academic achievement of linguistic-minority students, we need to investigate how and why the language and literacy practices and the contextualizing strategies utilized by the schooled and socially powerful have come to be touted as inherently superior and desirable in comparison to those practiced by lower-status cultural groups. It is important to understand that the practice of contextualizing language by relying chiefly on linguistic cues reflects Western European essayist or essay-text tradition.[27] Historically, oral language that resembles this type of written text organization has been heralded as more "logical" and desirable than less formal ways of structuring linguistic messages. Instead of recognizing the appropriateness of overtly explicit language (as well as its inappropriateness) in certain situations, the tendency has been to glorify this type of text organization. In the process, ideological claims are made about the essay-text's superior value, whether in speech or in writing, and these, in turn, become part of "'an armory of concepts, conventions and practices' that privilege one social formation as if it were natural, universal, or, at least, the end point of a normal developmental progression of cognitive skills."[28]

Thus, we strip so-called de-contextualized language of the almost magical properties attributed to it when we understand that, in reality, it refers to a speaker's and writer's ability to rely on dominant cultural knowledge and linguistic cues to render language *overtly* explicit and precise. As I have noted, researchers employ a variety of terms to describe oral and written language that relies primarily on linguistic cues for conveying meaning because shared meaning between interlocutors cannot be assumed. Consequently, linguistic messages must be elaborated on in an overtly precise and explicit manner and in an almost metacognitive fashion so that the risk of misinterpretation is minimized.

It is useful to dissect the concept of linguistically contextualized language (or "*de*-contextualized language," as it is more commonly referred to in the literature) to understand that its high value in part reflects the dominant culture's preference for structuring and contextualizing language in ways that minimize the interlocutors' joint creation and negotiation of meaning. In academic settings, high value is placed on producing text that is linguistically contextualized, thus reducing the importance of and need for human interaction and negotiation of meaning, especially when the interlocutors come from different class and ethnic groups.

Linguistically contextualized language therefore becomes a kind of lingua franca in academic domains. Certainly, the ability to contextualize language by relying chiefly on textual features, especially in academic domains where individuals are expected to communicate with distant and unknown audiences, is a desired one. A set of agreed-upon contextualizing conventions becomes necessary for successful communication to take place. Ana María Rodino accurately described the types of skills and conceptions of language that students must possess in order to produce this academic lingua franca:

> Being removed from the face-to-face setting, and assuming no prior knowledge on the part of unsupportive interlocutors, [linguistically] contextualized language requires anticipating recipient's needs/expectation; filling in background information; assessing message effectiveness on-line; self-monitoring and self-repair; careful planning to achieve a coherent whole; using precise lexical reference; controlling the complex syntax necessary to make explicit all relationships between ideas, and to sustain lexicalized cohesion across the whole text.[29]

It is important to recognize the value of this lingua franca in formal academic settings. However, I argue that instead of imbuing linguistically contextualized language with almost magical properties and denigrating students from cultural and social groups that generally do not rely on these types of contextualizing cues, it is important for educators of linguistic-minority students to clearly comprehend the sociopolitical dimensions of language and literacy teaching. By doing so, these educators can resist viewing the dominant groups' uses of language as inherently superior and desirable, and they can begin to identify ways for helping linguistic-minority students in the critical appropriation of academic discourses.

Language Devaluation and Resistance

In addition to the tendency to render the contextualizing strategies of the mainstream "invisible" (hence the term de-contextualized), there is also a tendency to make value judgments that adversely affect what is labeled *contextualized language* or language that is contextualized in paralinguistic ways and generally spoken by nonmainstream popula-tions. In other words, nonlinguistically contextualized language is often associated with the language variety spoken by groups that are generally relegated to the margins of the society. Thus, their linguistic production is not only devalued but also perceived as needing a "metamorphosis" of sorts into the standard discourse and text organization style, which is identified as *de*-contextualized.

The shift from a so-called context-bound to a seemingly *de*-contextu-alized discourse often involves psychological ramifications that can be far-reaching and yet are largely ignored by most teachers. For instance, the shift from a context-bound to a *de*-contextualized discourse can of-ten be accompanied by the development or exacerbation of linguistic insecurity, to the degree that students are encouraged to abandon or re-press their so-called context-bound language (which is usually devalued by the standard, middle-class-oriented curriculum). This form of lin-guistic coercion can produce linguistic resistance in students, who be-gin to experience antagonism toward the academic discourses they are often cajoled into learning.[30] If teachers do not fully understanding these psychological processes, which are generally shaped by compet-ing ideologies, they often fall into a binary position that does not bode well for a psychologically healthy pedagogy conducive to learning aca-demic discourses. This lack of understanding about student resistance often eclipses any possibility that teachers may detect linguistic resis-tance so they can mediate it and effectively teach the academic dis-courses while honoring the home discourses of their students.

I am reminded of a story told by Dell Hymes, a respected anthropolo-gist and educator, that illustrates my point. During the early sixties, while he was a professor at the Harvard Graduate School of Education, Hymes was recruited to help solve educational problems experienced by students in a Boston public elementary school located next to what was then the poorest and most dangerous housing project in Boston, popu-lated primarily by African Americans. The school's student population was almost 100 percent African American, but over 95 percent of the teachers and administrators were middle-class whites.

Hymes put into place mechanisms that encouraged and facilitated African American parents' involvement in the schools. These mecha-nisms also enabled teachers to familiarize themselves with the cultural backgrounds of the students they were teaching. Many African Ameri-can mothers became teachers' aides and helped bridge the gap between the school and the community. During one of the teacher-parent meet-ings, a well-meaning middle-class white teacher commented on her stu-dents' inability to learn standard English: "I have tried everything under the sun. I have gone downtown to buy colorful books, I have bought crayons, I use overheads, and these students still don't seem to be able to learn the standard." She was interrupted by an African American mother who was serving as an aide in her classroom: "Ma'am, I'm sorry, but I have to disagree with you. When I take these students outside for recess, and when they play school, when they role play the teacher, they speak exactly like you do."[31]

Here was a case in which students as young as seven or eight had, albeit unconsciously, begun to resist performing in the academic discourse in the classroom, although they were fully able to do so when the middle-class white teacher was absent. This example illustrates the fact that students whose language and culture are devalued by schools generally develop resistance mechanisms to protect their already fractured culture from the symbolic and real violence perpetrated against it by the middle-class white school culture.

The blind imposition of the so-called *de*-contextualized academic discourse not only reproduces the false assumption that academic discourses are not context bound, it also functions as a measure against which linguistic-minority students' contextualization of their language is devalued. This, in turn, may produce potentially serious psychological scars, even in students who fully master the academic discourses and go on to become highly successful professionals. For example, José Cárdenas, former director of the Intercultural Development Research Association in San Antonio, Texas, noted that his school experience was linguistically traumatic and left him with identifiable psychological scars: "I still remember it, not as an uncomfortable, unpleasant, or challenging situation, but, rather, as a traumatic, disconcerting, terrorizing experience."[32]

By not understanding the psychological ramifications of their pedagogy concerning the teaching of academic discourses to minority students, teachers more often than not blame the students for their failure. In the process, they fail to examine the erroneous assumptions that inform their pedagogy, which itself is predicated on the false dichotomy between context-bound and *de*-contextualized discourse. It is not true that minority students cannot learn standard academic discourses, as demonstrated by the young African American in the Boston public elementary school and by José Cárdenas. Instead, the problem often lies with the "traumatic, disconcerting, terrorizing experience" that generally leads minority students to find refuge in linguistic resistance to the imposition and promotion of what has been characterized by the dominant school culture as de-contextualized language.

As mentioned before, the tendency to label linguistically contextualized language as "*de*-contextualized" conjures up images of a mystical type of language, an entity in and of itself, which is touted as inherently superior to linguistic messages that may be entirely appropriate situationally but that rely on less academic ways of contextualizing. The theoretical framework that underlies my research effort is anchored in a critical sociocultural view of language and literacy. I find this approach useful for demystifying the notion of *de*-contextualized language while objectively understanding the academic communicative benefits for producing this type of language separately from its socially ascribed value. In other words, all language is "contextualized" in some manner, and the ways in which individuals decide to contextualize their utterances reflect, in part, the ways in which they have been socialized to construct utterances in various social situations. In some instances, individuals contextualize their language by relying chiefly on linguistic cues. In others, individuals contextualize their utterances by relying on extralinguistic cues, or they co-construct the context by depending on active listener interaction and collaboration.

Despite the importance attributed to the ability to linguistically contextualize discourse in academic settings, I have found no studies that examine the real-life linguistic contextualizing demands placed on bilingual Mexican American students in classrooms where teachers take a culturally sensitive approach to working with students. Research conducted on working-class African American students suggests that these students, in contrast to their middle-class white peers, produce language that is contextualized prosodically and is perceived by their teachers as less explicit, logical, and precise than language characterized as *de*-contextualized.[33] As a result, African American students (as is probably the case for other linguistic-minority students) are often misinterpreted and misassessed by their teachers. The few studies that have been conducted on bilingual students suggest that mainland working-class Puerto Rican students, like their African American peers, also rely chiefly on extralinguistic cues to contextualize their language.[34]

Teaching Academic Language to Linguistic-Minority Students

Given the importance accorded linguistically contextualized language in the exhibition of academic knowledge, as well as the likelihood that working-class Latino students (similar to other working-class students) may not develop middle-class academic contextualizing skills in the home, teachers must assist their linguistic-minority students in developing these skills at school. Thus, the challenge is not merely acquiring the English language per se. The real issue is the creation of appropriate pedagogical spaces where students can appropriate the middle-class-specific English discourse in all of its dimensions. For this reason, I believe that it is important to determine whether teachers' instructional demands and their evaluations of students' contextualizing strategies correspond to their actual classroom practices regarding the teaching and use of academic discourses.

Mexican American Students and Linguistically Contextualized Language

As discussed earlier, one reason for the differences in academic performance among Mexican Americans may be linked to their varying ability to "appropriately" contextualize language (oral and written) in academic ways—that is, to rely on linguistic cues to render their language overtly explicit and precise. The important work that Catherine Snow and her associates conducted with upper-class bilingual elementary students indicates that those who possess the ability to linguistically contextualize language in their primary language are soon able to transfer this ability to the second language.[35] This explanation lends support to the empirical work that shows that older immigrant students who are successful readers and writers in their first language are able to transfer and apply their literacy skills to the second language, once they achieve some minimal level of English proficiency.[36] I would argue that older working-class immigrant students not schooled in their primary language would not demonstrate the same ability to transfer discourse such as decontextualized correspondence does not apply to their linguistic reality. Class is usually a determining factor in the successful acquisition of English academic discourses.

It is interesting to note that it is precisely during the later elementary grades (fourth grade and beyond), when language (both oral and written) becomes more linguistically contextualized, that Mexican American students begin to fall behind in school.[37] As Snow and her associates suggested, "The reading and writing tasks expected of children in the later elementary, middle and high school grades cannot be accomplished without both productive and receptive [linguistic contextualizing language] skills."[38] Despite these findings, little has been done to study the actual language demands placed on working-class Mexican American bilingual students to linguistically contextualize their language (in both English and Spanish).

In the chapters that follow, I discuss the academic discourse used by working-class Mexican American students and their teacher in one fifth-grade English and Spanish bilingual classroom. Specifically, I examine one bilingual teacher's efforts to create participation structures that elicit students' production of linguistically contextualized language. I also analyze the students' ability to linguistically contextualize their language in both English and Spanish in the classroom during normally occurring lessons. Although the student sample in this instance is Mexican American,[39] I argue that similar language patterns possibly hold true for other working-class linguistic-minority students and students who speak nonstandard English.

Research in bilingual and linguistic-minority education has not thoroughly addressed the issue of linguistic conflict, although some efforts have been made to explain the resistance of linguistic-minority students to learning a second language and culture.[40] Much of the literature continues to treat the phenomena of acquiring English as a second language and acquiring standard dialects as apolitical undertakings that are relatively easy if students are cognitively capable language learners.

It is my hope that the information contained in the six chapters of this book will serve to advance the present theoretical debate concerning what constitutes academic discourses and how they are (mis)taught in schools, particularly to working-class linguistic-minority students.

2 Language and Ideology: The (Il)literacy of Linguistic-Minority Students

Much of the work that examines linguistic-minority students' language and literacy practices in the classroom has tended to take a cultural deficit or cultural mismatch perspective. Later in this chapter, I discuss these perspectives in greater depth. I argue that rather than subscribing to models of cultural difference and incongruence, researchers should develop a more comprehensive theoretical framework that takes into account the real ideological dimensions of linguistic-minority education. As I suggested in the previous chapter, the teaching of dominant cultural and linguistic bases (such as linguistically contextualized language) is not a politically neutral undertaking. All teaching and learning take place in real classrooms that often mirror the asymmetrical power relations among members of subordinate and dominant culture groups in the greater society. Given that, it is important for educators to more fully understand how to negotiate real and potential ideological tensions, which often take the form of students' linguistic resistance in the classroom. The real goal is not to attempt to suffocate these tensions because, in most cases, they are inevitable. In fact, the attempt to suffocate ideological tensions is part of a process in which the dominant ideology falsifies reality by pretending that ideological tensions no longer exist. The important pedagogical strategy is not to do away with the tensions but to recognize that they exist and to try to understand those ideological elements that produced the tensions, so that they can be negotiated in a democratic and safe manner.

I also argue that a critical sociocultural perspective of language and literacy leads to a more comprehensive model for understanding the political and ideological dimensions of teaching academic discourses to Mexican American and other low-status linguistic-minority students. A critical sociocultural view explores the relationships between sociocultural experiences and language and literacy practices, as proposed by Paulo Freire, Lev Vygotsky, and James Gee, among others.[1] Although the acquisition of academic discourse and linguistically contextualizing strategies among Mexican American students is my primary interest, the discussion that follows focuses on the language use of students from a number of linguistic-minority groups (including African Americans) that traditionally have also fared poorly in school. I refer to specific studies of Mexican Americans and other Latinos whenever possible, and I also cite studies dealing with other working-class linguistic-minority groups as well as middle-class white students.

One important feature of a critical sociocultural view of language and literacy is its recognition of the culture-specific nature of definitions of literacy (for example, the use of and value ascribed to linguistically contextualized conventions). In addition, a critical sociocultural perspective posits that literacy is more than the ability to read and write; it also involves a culturally prescribed way of *thinking about* and *using* language (both oral and written). Thus, the concept of multiple literacies is not merely accepted but also embraced to the extent that members of different social and cultural groups may all read and write (decode and encode) but utilize language (oral and written) for different purposes, in different contexts, and from different positions of power vis-à-vis the dominant culture. Similarly, the ways in which people contextualize their utterances also reflect culturally prescribed views of what constitutes human communication and how one goes about effectively communicating with others.

Another important feature of a sociocultural view of literacy is that it recognizes language learning as being simultaneously a *sociocultural* phenomenon and a *cognitive* phenomenon. Learning is influenced both by social interaction within a culture and by individual participation in the learning process. Individuals acquire literacy skills through the exercise of culture-specific practices. It is only after successive experiences that individuals eventually develop self-evaluative and self-regulatory skills. Thus, the language and literacy practices valued by particular groups or cultures and the abilities resulting from those practices are instilled in and replicated by each generation through either formal or informal methods of instruction. Clearly then, strategies for assisting individual members from nonmainstream cultural groups to linguistically contextualize their language necessarily require mentoring or apprenticing by more capable others so that student internalization occurs.

The Political and Ideological
Dimensions of Culture

It is important to point out that in my discussion of a critical sociocultural theory of language and literacy, the term *culture* is not used in the
traditional, restricted sense, which renders it devoid of its dynamic, ideological, and political dimensions. Usually, *culture* is considered syn-
onymous with *ethnic culture*, rather than as "the representation of lived
experiences, material artifacts and practices *forged within the unequal
and dialectical relations* that different groups establish in a given society
at a particular point in historical time."[2] I find the latter definition of culture, which recognizes the asymmetrical power relations among cultures, more comprehensive and informative. Moreover, I believe it provides the tools we need to understand that unless we identify the
political and ideological dimensions of culture and the subsequent unequal status attributed to members of different ethnic groups, it may appear that the language and literacy practices of certain groups are, indeed, superior to those of low-status ethnic and social groups (which are
perceived at best to be "different" or at worst as "deviant").

In reality, values placed on language and literacy practices reflect the
greater society's socioeconomic and political hierarchy. That is, the language and literacy practices of dominant cultural groups are usually
deemed more valuable and desirable than those of groups that are socially, economically, and politically less powerful.[3] This social reality is
clearly evident in the preference for linguistically contextualized language in academic settings. Yet a more accurate and academically honest definition of culture would remind us that, despite social preferences
and prejudices, the language practices of linguistic-minority and lower-
status populations are inherently equal to those of higher-status or
dominant groups. Such an appraisal of language and literacy practices
would also help educators distinguish between the intrinsic value and
the socially ascribed value of particular practices.

An emphasis on the political and ideological dimensions of culture
also challenges the common assumption that the language and literacy
practices of lower-status populations magically spring from the earth
and are solely the results of an *ethnic* cultural lifestyle, separate and
apart from the sociopolitical and economic realities that impact and
shape them. For example, if a particular ethnic group has (1) been historically stigmatized and perceived or treated as low-status, (2) developed, in the process, antagonistic relations with members of the dominant cultural group in a society, and (3) been prevented (either
consciously or unconsciously) from participating in practices that promote the acquisition of language and literacy knowledge and skills val-

ued by the dominant society, the group often develops alternative language and literacy practices that help its members survive. This survival mechanism is not solely a cultural phenomenon; it is also an ideological and political process that should be recognized when discussing the group's practices. The challenge for educators is to understand the ways in which different cultural practices, particularly with respect to literacy events, are sometimes used as a form of resistance to the perceived and real oppressive conditions and how resistance can be used pedagogically as a tool for literacy development.

The Political and Ideological Dimensions of Cognition

Even when we discuss language and literacy learning as a cognitive occurrence, it is necessary to acknowledge the ideological and political influences on cognitive formation. This type of macro-understanding would help educators grasp more fully the possible effects of unequal power relations among groups in a society, as well as the possible implications this power asymmetry may have at the classroom level and the adverse effects it can have on learning and teaching. For example, a conventional sociocultural theory of literacy learning posits that under ideal conditions, teacher and learner engage in amicable social interactions that permit the learner to participate actively in her or his own learning and ensure that successful teaching and learning can take place. In addition, teachers are expected to mentor and model desired behavior, language use, and a particular worldview until the students have internalized these skills and are capable of exhibiting them without assistance. However, educators must avoid a paternalistic mentoring that purports to respect linguistic-minority students' literacy practices by engaging in a form of condescension whereby the celebration of these practices ultimately devalues them.

If the sociocultural and political reality is one in which teacher and learner are antagonistic toward each other—if the teacher unconsciously or consciously resists mentoring students perceived as deficient and if students, in turn, reject the devaluation of their existing language and literacy skills and the imposition of the dominant culture's language and literacy practices—very little teaching and learning will take place. Effective mentorship can only occur when pedagogical spaces are created that enable students to move from *object* to *subject* position and become active participants in their own learning.[4]

This more comprehensive and political definition of the term *culture* needs to be kept in mind when applying a sociocultural view of language and literacy. In fact, acknowledging and understanding the ideological and political dimensions of culture are precisely what render this particular perspective "critical." Too often, even proponents of a more traditional sociocultural view stop short of discussing the ideological and political dimensions of the theoretical framework. Frequently, in fact, when proponents of this perspective argue that it is necessary to consider the sociocultural context, they refer to the immediate classroom context or to the immediate ethnic community (neighborhood), while disarticulating the classroom context on the ethnic community from the larger social order that influences, shapes, and maintains the asymmetrical distribution of cultural goods. The sociocultural net must be cast more broadly since it is also necessary to acknowledge the impact of political and ideological realities on culture formation and maintenance; any discussion of linguistic-minority students' language and literacy practices must take into account the larger sociopolitical context in which these practices have developed and in which teacher and student negotiate the maintenance of primary discourses and the acquisition of the dominant culture's secondary discourses.

A Critical Sociocultural View of Literacy

James Gee's concept of "Discourse" is particularly illustrative of the sociocultural (and ideological and political) nature of teaching and learning and quite relevant to my discussion of linguistic-minority students' academic discourse acquisition.[5] In fact, he correctly pointed out the prominence of social and political dimensions of language and literacy learning when he argued that "the focus of literacy studies cannot be, and ought not to be, on language, or even literacy itself as traditionally construed. Rather, the focus must be on the social practices that encompass the language and literacy practices."[6] This implies that in order for an individual to acquire particular language and literacy skills, she or he must be apprenticed into a particular discourse by a more knowledgeable "teacher" or mentor. Gee's concept of "Discourse" is particularly useful for better understanding the issue of contextualizing conventions and their relation to literacy achievement. This concept of discourse captures the significance of sociopolitical context and requires apprenticeship for a student to become a capable user of language (both oral and written): "A Discourse is a socially accepted association among ways of using language, of thinking, feeling, believing, valuing, and of acting that can be used to identify oneself as a member of a socially meaningful group or 'social network,' or to signal (that one is playing) a socially meaningful 'role.'"[7]

Gee likened a discourse to an "identity kit" of sorts that a participant adopts. In order to enact the adopted identity, the participant must behave and use language in ways identified as appropriate within the particular discourse. A person does not come to master language outside real-life contexts. That is, one reads, writes, and speaks for real purposes, and this linguistic performance reflects the context in which the speaker/writer finds her- or himself, as well as her or his role within that particular context. The identity kit includes ways of using language that reflect a particular role and worldview or ideology. Examples of discourses include "(enacting) being an American or a Russian, a man or a woman, a member of a certain socioeconomic class, a factory worker or a boardroom executive, a doctor, or a hospital patient, a teacher, an administrator, or a student, a student of physics . . . or a regular at a local bar."[8] Thus, discourses are representative of multiple realities, which also produce multiple identities that may or may not be in conflict with one another. What is important is that the cultural capital is often asymmetrically distributed to different discourses and that the currency of each social location often determines how a particular discourse is valued or devalued. What educators cannot afford to do is to ignore the multiplicity of social locations and the roles these locations play in identity formation. Since identity is intimately tied to cultural and literacy practices (particularly those practices involved in the reading of the world), educators must not only respect these practices by using them as an integral part of their pedagogy, they must also avoid any intervention leading to the devaluation of the students' cultural and literacy practices. Devaluation often triggers resistance, and in such cases, education becomes a process through which linguistic-minority students experience subordination in the very act of learning to read and write and in the acquisition of academic discourses. Although acquiring the academic discourses is an important educational goal, this acquisition should never sacrifice linguistic-minority students' primary discourses, which are the only means through which they make sense of their world, culture, and history.

The Acquisition of Secondary Dominant Discourses

Gee posited two basic categories of discourse—the primary and the secondary. He also presented the concept of powerful or critical discourses, which will be discussed later in this chapter. Primary discourses are the "identity kits" (for example, ways of using language, values, worldview, and so forth) acquired during the initial socialization within the family or other primary socializing unit. The primary discourse serves as a foundation for the later acquisition of secondary discourses.

Secondary discourses are "identity kits" acquired later, in secondary institutions such as the schools, workplaces, stores, government offices,

and churches, where contact can no longer be assumed to occur between "intimates." Secondary discourses all build on and extend, to
varying degrees, the language and ideologies acquired as part of the primary discourse. It is important to point out that some primary discourses may be more conducive to the acquisition of certain secondary
discourses. Thus, a primary discourse acquired through a middle-class
home socialization often facilitates the acquisition of a secondary discourse acquired through schools, the reason being that schools reflect
and refract a middle-class reality that is usually a yardstick against
which other primary discourses (lower-class, racial, and ethnic) are
measured.

Consequently, I believe that it is a great advantage when any secondary discourse is compatible with the primary one. Students whose
primary discourse more closely reflects that of the school are often erroneously perceived as being more capable than peers socialized in less-
similar primary discourses. This usually occurs when middle-class white
students come to school with contextualizing strategies and notions
about linguistic explicitness and preciseness that reflect the practices
and preferences of the dominant culture. These students are likely to be
perceived as more capable and intelligent, even though, in reality, by
virtue of their ascribed membership in the dominant cultural group in
the society, they simply have had more opportunities to acquire and
practice the socially valued language skills. By contrast, students from
linguistic-minority groups who come to school with valuable knowledge
and skills but who do not exhibit their knowledge in linguistically "appropriate" ways are often considered less competent and intelligent by
their teachers.

In fact, it is often suggested that linguistic-minority children perform
poorly in school because they lack particular knowledge bases and thinking (cognitive) skills. However, I would argue that linguistic-minority
children may experience difficulties in school not because they lack particular knowledge and thinking abilities but because they may use linguistic structures and styles (to exhibit their knowledge and skills) that
are not respected, valued, or understood by teachers. For this reason, we
urgently need more studies that investigate why teachers do not respect
or value linguistic-minority students' repertoire of discourse skills and
knowledge bases.[9] Through such studies, teachers can begin to acquire
the necessary skills to unveil the dominant ideology that informs their erroneous assumptions about the superior valuation of so-called *de*-con-
textualized discourse. And through rigorous studies, teachers can begin
to understand students' resistance to their classroom practices, as well as
the possible roles they themselves may play in exacerbating the teacher-
student antagonism that leads to an increase in the students' resistance

to the academic discourse. In short, increasing teachers' political clarity could help them understand the context in which they teach academic discourses and also offer them better means to reflect on questions such as whether and why it is important to explicitly teach academic discourses, how to teach them, to whom, and against whom.[10]

By developing political clarity, educators should be better able to understand why the young African American student at a Boston public elementary school, mentioned earlier, willfully refused to emulate her middle-class white teacher's speech patterns. In addition, increased political clarity should also help teachers understand their role in creating school contexts that are "traumatic, disconcerting, terrorizing experience[s]."[11] Increased political clarity should also propel teachers to critically investigate and identify the linguistic items and discourse mechanisms that are valued by the school so they can explicitly teach them to their students without devaluing the primary discourses that students bring into their classrooms.[12]

Although I agree that primary and secondary discourses are best mastered when learners are informally enculturated or apprenticed into them, I must point out that enculturation should never create structures whereby minority students are deculturated from their primary cultural sources. Acquisition and learning require access that is psychologically harmless, something that is absent in models of enculturation that subsume deculturation. In other words, the enculturation process should be additive and build upon the cultural capital the students bring to school. Thus, enculturation into the dominant discourse should necessarily be a process through which students "interrogate and selectively appropriate those aspects of the dominant culture that will provide them with the basis for defining and transforming, rather than merely serving, the wider social order."[13] This necessarily requires that teachers and students be fully conscious of their intentions to teach and master the dominant culture's secondary discourses.

Acquisition Versus Learning: Linguistic-Minority Students' Need for Both

In order for a student to became nativelike in a secondary discourse, he or she must be informally socialized into its use, in addition to being formally and explicitly taught. This requires that teachers distinguish between the two ways of gaining new knowledge—by learning and by acquiring, as eloquently discussed by Gee:

> [Learning refers to] a process that involves conscious knowledge gained through teaching (though not necessarily from someone officially desig-

nated a teacher) or through certain life-experiences that trigger conscious reflection. This teaching or reflection involves explanation and analysis, that is, breaking down the thing to be learned into its analytic parts. It inherently involves attaining, along with the matter being taught, some degree of meta-knowledge about the matter.

[Acquisition refers to] a process of acquiring something subconsciously by exposure to models, a process of trial and error, and practice within social groups, without formal teaching. It happens in natural settings which are meaningful and functional in the sense that acquirers know that they need to acquire the thing they are exposed to in order to function and they in fact want to so function. This is how most people come to control their first language.[14]

In essence, both ways of gaining knowledge differ in terms of students' level of consciousness or purposefulness in acquiring new secondary discourses. Although it may be true that students who are informally socialized into new discourses are better performers that those who are formally and explicitly taught, I contend that linguistic-minority students need to both learn and acquire dominant discourses. Not only do they need to display nativelike mastery and comfort when utilizing secondary discourses, they also need to possess explicit and critical awareness of their own learning and acquisition of new worldviews and ways of using language.

In order to promote both types of new knowledge gains, optimal classroom conditions would offer learning contexts in which students are both explicitly taught *and* informally socialized into new secondary discourses by teachers conscious of their role as cultural mentors. The actual content of a discourse (such as ways of using and contextualizing language, behaving, and believing) is mastered by individuals in situations in which a teacher (or a more knowledgeable other) explicitly and implicitly assists the individuals in both learning and acquiring skills and knowledge bases necessary for full membership in a discourse. For example, in a graduate school setting, an ideal adviser will support and assist a student in becoming a full-fledged member of a particular discourse or discipline, such as sociology. Thus, the ideal sociology adviser will not only explicitly share knowledge of the content area with the student but also implicitly model how to dress, behave, and think like an "acceptable" sociologist. Ultimately, it is the graduate student's responsibility to make choices regarding what aspects of the discourse to acquire or ignore. However, what is important is that the student has been provided with the necessary "insider" cultural information. Similarly, in an elementary classroom setting, teachers can both implicitly model new communicative strategies, thinking processes, and worldviews and, at some point, make the implicit explicit by engaging the students in discussion around the significance of adding to one's repertoire new language and thinking skills, such as linguistically contextualizing conventions. The goal, however, is to always maintain the students' epistemological curiosity, without which learning is nearly impossible.

Powerful Discourses and an Ideal Definition of Literacy

Another concept that helps illustrate the importance of explicit and metacognitive discourse teaching and learning is referred to as "powerful discourse," which involves the acquisition of metacognitive skills that allow an individual to stand apart from a particular primary or secondary discourse in order to analyze and critique it. Acquisition of secondary discourses does not automatically guarantee that an individual will develop the metacognitive skills necessary to critique and analyze primary and secondary discourses. Therefore, it is necessary to ensure the learning of such skills by explicitly teaching them and by creating classroom contexts that are safe and conducive to critique, analysis, and reflection.

Returning to the sociologist example, the ideal teacher would make sure that her or his student has acquired the necessary knowledge, skills, and predisposition to become an acceptable sociologist and then, at some point, would also help the student reveal, articulate, and critique the tacit "rules" of the secondary discourse of sociology being acquired. Ideally, this would produce a student who is knowledgeable and capable of functioning as an acceptable sociologist but also critically cognizant of the particular discourse's implicit rules and ideological perspectives, as well as the limitations and contradictions found in discourses. In addition, the student would be capable of comparing and contrasting congruent as well as oppositional discourses.

An ideal definition of literacy would thus move beyond mere mastery of a secondary discourse to include mastery of multiple secondary discourses and the ability to critique the primary and secondary discourses from a variety of ideological (discourse) standpoints. Mastery of powerful discourses would enable students to develop metacognitive and analytic skills so they can become critical thinkers, rather than blindly and complacently accepting secondary discourses and their underlying ideologies and values. The importance of mastering powerful discourses is particularly relevant when discussing students who are members of linguistic-minority and other lower-status groups.

Therefore, instead of imposing as superior the secondary discourses of the dominant culture (such as linguistically contextualized language) and requiring that students discard primary discourses that are less socially valued, it would be more intellectually honest for schools to assist students in the critical appropriation of as many secondary discourses as possible, while maintaining their primary discourses. In fact, this is precisely what happens to middle- and upper-class students. Schooling is a process through which they add secondary discourses to their primary discourse. They are never required to do away with or sacrifice their primary discourse. Unfortunately, that same pedagogy does not apply to primary discourses that are devalued by virtue of their association with a lower class, ethnicity, race, or gender. Critical appropriation of secondary discourses, particularly dominant secondary discourses, would enable linguistic-minority and other lower-status students to understand the strengths and weaknesses of all acquired discourses. Ideally, students would resist accepting any discourse as innately superior or inferior and instead strategically step in and out of discourses at will. This would certainly represent a pedagogical process that not only empowers linguistic-minority students but also enables them to find their voices both in their primary and secondary discourses.

Ideology, Teaching, and Language

Thus far, the discussion of discourses clearly illustrates the ideological and political nature of language and literacy teaching and learning. The theoretical framework presented demonstrates that coming to master a discourse is not a politically neutral undertaking. The apprenticeship process itself illustrates the political dimensions of language and literacy teaching and learning. In order for effective apprenticing to take place, some sort of supportive mentoring must occur between the "teacher" and the "students," even when the two parties belong to social and cultural groups that have antagonistic relations. In addition, the degree of value associated with various primary and secondary discourses reflects the asymmetrical power relations among cultural groups in the greater society. Any superordinate value placed on certain discourses over others clearly reflects greater sociopolitical realities rather than the inherent qualities of a given discourse per se.[15]

Educators need to be especially cognizant of the ideological and political aspects of working with subordinated linguistic-minority groups. Though they should be challenging, teachers should also be constantly vigilant lest unexamined and classist linguistic and social biases prevent them from objectively and strategically assisting and encouraging their students in maintaining their primary discourse while acquiring various academic secondary discourses. An educator's critical stance necessarily requires the interpretation of current discussions regarding linguistic-minority students' language performance in schools.

The next section presents an opportunity to critically examine (or re-examine) one leading explanation regarding linguistic-minority students' academic underachievement: the cultural difference or incongruence theory. I will discuss two bodies of linguistic research that explicitly or implicitly subscribe to a cultural difference or incongruence explanation. The two bodies of research are: (1) classic ethnographic studies that examine linguistic-minority students' participation and communication style differences in the classroom; and (2) descriptive studies that specifically examine student use of linguistically contextualized language (or *de*-contextualized language, as it is referred to in the literature) in classroom settings. The ethnographic studies discussed consist of classic research that identifies minority student participation and communication practices deemed sufficiently "different" (from mainstream practices) so as to create classroom conditions under which teacher and student miscommunication is likely to occur, resulting in student underachievement. The *de*-contextualized language studies describe ethnic and class differences in students' ability to produce oral and written *de*-contextualized language.

Although this second body of work does not explicitly subscribe to a cultural difference or incongruence model, many researchers attribute student *de*-contextualizing language differences to culturally distinct text-organizing strategies and contextualizing styles.

Cultural Incongruence and Mismatch:
An Ideological Trap

As mentioned earlier, despite the obvious sociocultural dimensions of linguistic-minority language and literacy teaching and learning, much of the relevant literature fails to discuss the political and ideological tensions inherent in such work. Sadly enough, work that subscribes (either explicitly or implicitly) to a sociocultural framework often fails to address the sociopolitical and ideological dimensions of teaching and learning. For example, much of the sociocultural research that examines the academic discourse and interaction patterns of linguistic-minority students in U.S. schools yet, surprisingly, assumes an almost apolitical stance falls under the rubric of cultural incongruence literature. This body of literature grows out of cultural difference theory, which attributes the academic and communicative difficulties of lower-status groups to cultural and linguistic incongruence, or discontinuities between the groups' primary discourses and the secondary discourses expected by the schools.

A number of classic ethnographic studies document the culturally "different" communication practices in classrooms where students and teachers may speak the same language (English) but use it in different and "incongruent" ways. I review four key classic studies to illustrate significant political and ideological aspects of literacy and language instruction that too often go unreported while the causes of underachievement are chiefly and erroneously attributed to cultural "differences" and "incongruence."

Depoliticizing Historical Subjugation: Lessons from Present-Day Communication and Literacy Practices

Shirley Heath's classic ethnographic study illustrated a situation in which academic difficulties were attributed to cultural (socioeconomic and racial) differences, yet the discussion was not presented against a macro sociopolitical and historical backdrop.[16] Her work focused on the language and literacy practices of working-class African Americans and white Americans and contrasted them with those practices expected by teachers. She compared three communities of different ethnic and/or socioeconomic status, suggesting that patterns of language and literacy use differed in each of the three communities and were reflected in three general patterns of school achievement:

1. Middle-class children of teachers were found to be the highest achieving in school.

2. White students of low socioeconomic status were found to begin failing after second or third grade.

3. African American children of low socioeconomic status were reported to experience academic failure throughout elementary school.

Although the parents in both low-socioeconomic-status groups were literate in the sense that they could read and write at least at a basic level, they had little opportunity in their everyday lives to use the reading and writing language skills taught in school. Although this was not discussed by Heath, African Americans' lack of opportunity to practice the reading and writing skills taught in school may reflect their general lack of access to the middle-class white contexts in which academic literacy skills are used. This lack of access also reflects our still highly segregated society, which is often mirrored in our schools. Given the highly segregated nature of U.S. society, is not surprising to find that the functions of literacy in both African American and white communities at a low socioeconomic level are different from the functions of literacy in a middle-class mainstream (teacher) community. As a result of the sociopolitical specificities experienced by each low-status group, different outlooks on literacy and distinctive communicative skills specific to these uses of literacy have emerged. However, the emergence of distinctive literacy patterns is not endemic to race but is the by-product of a racist society. In other words, African Americans who have full access to middle-class white academic discourse due to their social class may not necessarily exhibit literacy patterns that are attributed to their racial makeup. They may often easily acquire the middle-class white discourse (as exemplified in Heath's sample of African American mainstream teachers.)

Thus, in my opinion, Heath's analysis, although informative, failed to address the conditions of social apartheid that shape literacy practices in African American communities. What we need to understand is that the different literacy functions in these communities are not merely social in nature; many also result from the oppressive racial segregation that shapes and conditions these functions. Nevertheless, Heath's work offered many useful findings, such as the fact that in certain African American communities, reading is generally done in groups and rarely in isolation. Heath reported that "in short, written information never stood alone in Trackton [the low-socioeconomic-status African American community]; it was reshaped and reworded into an 'oral' mode and reading is not an individual pursuit nor is it considered to have intellectual, aesthetic, or critical rewards."[17]

Although this finding is useful in that it may help teachers better understand the language and literacy dynamics in some African American communities, it would, in the long run, be a real disservice to teachers and to African Americans if we were to remain on the surface of the information provided by Heath. What must be fully understood is the text that undergirds the African American social orientation to reading. Heath failed to discuss the fact that below the surface social orientation to reading lies a subtext that is the by-product of the U.S. racist fabric that robbed African Americans of their human rights to literacy through discriminatory laws forbidding them to read.

After these laws were repealed, the institutional roots of racism reimposed themselves in new and more subtle forms, which continue to deny African Americans access to literate academic discourses. Hence, it is probable that reading in groups represents a vestige of slavery, when few African Americans could read and those who had mastered the reading process would share their knowledge of the text with those who were forced to remain illiterate. This trait is still common in societies where illiteracy rates remain high. Thus, I believe that reading for the group may have a great deal more to do with the legacy of slavery than with working-class African American culture per se. By not deconstructing how the structure of racism may have impacted literacy development among African Americans, Heath, in fact, collapsed the political into the cultural and erased the political. By viewing everything through a cultural lens only, she avoided making bare the power asymmetry that has informed and continues to sustain the antagonistic relationship between African Americans and the dominant white group.

That the functions of literacy have more to do with subordinated status than with depoliticized notions of "culture" is supported by the evidence showing that the functions of literacy were also found to be different in the low-socioeconomic situation of the white community. Although mainstream reading and reading-related activities reportedly occurred more frequently in this socioeconomic and ethnic community, the purpose of reading differed because it focused on "the truth." Children came to perceive a book as an author's nonfictional account or a factual account to be learned and not critiqued or questioned. The tendency in this community was to interpret children's fictionalized accounts as lies; as a result, imagination and creativity were discouraged, and children were encouraged to repeat only facts. Again, a surface-feature interpretation of this work could lead an educator to view this focus on "truth" as a sole result of a particular cultural way of life (such as a white, southern fundamentalist religious upbringing). Little effort was made to problematize the phenomenon—that is, to engage in some sort of class analysis and to question why it was that the low-status white students (and their parents) in this study exhibited self-limiting behaviors and continued to view texts as authority. In this particular case study, the linking of socially attributed low status with the group's acceptance of that status and the religious ideology that supported acceptance and unquestioning behaviors should have been discussed. There is a need for more research that chronicles the differential socialization of working-class students in the schools, churches, and other institutions that anesthetizes (at least on the surface) these students' ability to question their lot in life. Instead, they view learning as getting the "right" answer and reading as "barking" at print.

According to Heath, the problems that low-socioeconomic-level African American and white children encountered in school were directly related to (1) the language and literacy practices required in the school but not present in their homes, and (2) the inability of school personnel to recognize many of the language and literacy skills the children of low socioeconomic status brought to school with them. In summary, the types of literate thinking skills developed by children in the two low-socioeconomic communities did not coincide with those expected, and they were not exhibited in ways readily discerned by mainstream teachers.

Though Heath's findings certainly captured the language and literacy "differences" in the homes of low-status whites and blacks in comparison to those of teachers, her analysis did not go beyond describing the "here and now" practices of these groups, dislodged from their sociopolitical and historical context. It is unfortunate that Heath did not weave through her study a more in-depth sociopolitical history of the three groups—a concept that she briefly discussed in the prologue of her book, where she acknowledged the limitations of ethnographic work and recognized the importance of historical influences. According to Heath,

> Anthropologists study social life as and where it is lived through the median of a particular social group, but the ethnographic present never remains as it is described, *nor does the description of the current times fully capture the influence and force of history on the present.* . . . It is because one of the communities of focus in the book is Black and the other is White that the social history of such communities in the Piedmont region is especially critical to understanding the ethnographic present."[18]

Even though she recognized the importance of historicity in ethnographic studies, Heath failed to incorporate an in-depth historical analysis that made sense of her present description of these communities. It is unfortunate that she failed to situate her descriptions of the three groups' language and literacy practices against the history of subordination that shaped and continues to shape these practices in the first place.

Equalizing Asymmetrical Power Relations: Creating Pedagogical Spaces for Sharing Ways of Knowing and Speaking

A critical sociocultural and political discussion is similarly absent in other classic classroom ethnographies. These studies have described language and literacy practices of linguistic-minority students identified as culturally incongruent to those practices expected by classroom teachers. The research discussed in the following passages examined cultural differences in student and teacher language use and interaction style in the classroom and the communication problems that developed because of these cultural incongruencies. Unfortunately, the researchers limited themselves to attributing the communication and academic problems to culture-specific practices that did not happen to "match" the practices of the dominant cultural groups. Academic failure was thus attributed chiefly to the fact that linguistic-minority children often came to school with language and literacy skills that went unrecognized by teachers because of differences in surface features of the ways students verbally demonstrated or exhibited knowledge. However, the question I consider key—why middle-class white teachers consistently and automatically undervalue and disrespect "different" communication practices and skills—has seldom been addressed critically and explicitly in the literature.

While studying the classroom language behavior of Warm Springs, Oregon, Native American children, Susan Philips reported that teachers perceived the children as lacking appropriate language and interaction skills.[19] The teachers' major complaints emphasized the children's silent behavior and what they perceived to be a lack of cooperation in the classroom. Interested in learning why Native American children chose to speak in certain classroom situations and not in others, Philips compared an all-Indian class to an all-white norm group to identify those classroom situations in which the Native American students' verbal participation was minimal. She then examined whether the Native Americans were similarly silent in comparable situations in the home and community. Although the study did not sufficiently describe the types of verbal interactions in the community, Philips asserted that "Native American children's verbal interactions outside the classroom indicate a controlled and pro ductive use of linguistic rules that is manifested infrequently in classroom utterances, indicating that the appropriate social conditions for speech use (in the classroom) from the Indians' point of view, are lacking."[20]

Thus, it was not so much that the children were generally nonverbal but rather that they were nonverbal in situations that they perceived as inappropriate for speaking. When the teachers took it upon themselves to create learning contexts that resembled those in the Native American community that encouraged talk and active participation, they found the students responded more actively.

Similar teacher "confusion" regarding linguistic-minority students' language practices in the classroom were reported by Katheryn Hu-Pei Au and Jana Mason.[21] In this case, the linguistic-minority group studied were native Hawaiian children. The researchers examined the children's participation practices, which were described by teachers as unruly and without educational value. Au found that the children's preferred language style in the classroom was linked to an adult style of interaction called "talk story," which was used in their homes and community. She described talk story as a major speech event in the Hawaiian community, in which individuals speak almost simultaneously and little attention is given to taking turns. This phenomenon was described by Karen Watson-Gegeo and Stephen T. Boggs as a high proportion of turns involving joint performance and cooperative production of responses by two or more persons: "Turn taking is negotiated among the children in a manner generally tending to sustain joint performance through the involvement of others, and not in a manner which allocates exclusive speaking rights to one person, as so often happens in the classroom lessons."[22]

Apparently, this practice inhibits students from speaking out individually because of their familiarity with and preference for simultaneous group discussion. Because the mainstream teachers were unfamiliar with talk story and failed to recognize its value, much class time was spent either silencing the children or prodding unwilling individuals to speak. Needless to say, very little class time was dedicated to instruction. More important, the children were constrained and not allowed to demonstrate their abilities as speakers and possessors of knowledge. Because the students did not exhibit their skills in mainstream, accepted ways (for example, by competing as individuals for the floor), they were prevented from exhibiting knowledge through their preferred interaction style. However, once the children's interaction style was incorporated into classroom lessons, time on task increased and students' performance on standardized reading tests subsequently improved.

Like Heath, the ethnographers in these two studies examined language and literacy practices identified as problematic by classroom teachers, traced the practices to the ethnic/linguistic community, and provided classroom recommendations for re-creating learning environments in which students could best display their academic and linguistic skills. Thus, Philips discovered that the Native American children in her study were considerably more verbal in certain community settings than in the classroom. Her educational recommendations included creating learning environments in the classroom that incorporated aspects of the community events in which the students were observed to be more verbal and active. In her Hawaiian work, Au discovered that a "talk story" manner of discussing was present in the community during adult discussions. Although there were no events in the greater community that encouraged this type of simultaneous group discussion and included children (they did exist for adults),[23] teachers and researchers attempted to create learning situations during classroom lessons that would allow the children to speak and respond to their teachers' questions jointly.

Across the ethnographic studies discussed, the researchers diagnosed the communication difficulties as being cultural or linguistic in nature. That is, the problems the children encountered in effectively communicating their intent and the difficulties the teachers reported in getting their students to behave and speak in classroom-appropriate ways were explained as cultural or linguistic misunderstandings. It is interesting to note that many of the studies also inadvertently failed to describe the unequal power relations existing between mainstream teachers and low-status linguistic-minority students. These studies described classrooms in which teachers, at least initially, imposed participation structures and language functions on their students. With the assistance of the researchers, the teachers in all these studies learned to negotiate with students rules regarding acceptable classroom language use and behavior.

Thus, these studies, in essence, captured the successful negotiation of power relations, which resulted in higher student academic achievement and increased teacher effectiveness. Yet there was little explicit discussion in these studies of the greater sociopolitical reality that renders it perfectly normal for teachers automatically to disregard and disrespect low-status students' language forms and preferences and to allow antagonistic relations to foment until the teachers are presented with empirical evidence that legitimizes the students' practices. Instead, the focus of most of these studies rested entirely on the cultural and linguistic congruence of the new instruction and not on its humanizing and democratic effects. Ana María Villegas accurately critiqued the cultural congruence literature when she stated: "It is simplistic to claim that differences in language used at home and in school are the root of the widespread academic problems of minority children. Admittedly, differences do exist, and they can create communication difficulties in the classroom for both teachers and students. Even so, those *differences in language must be viewed in the context of a broader struggle for power within a stratified society.*"[24]

Despite the focus on the cultural and linguistic, rather than the political, dimensions of pedagogy, some effort has been made to link culturally and linguistically congruent teaching practices with the equalization of classroom power relations. For example, Katheryn Hu-Pei Au and Jana Mason explained that "one means of achieving congruence in lessons may be to *seek a balance between the interactional rights of teachers and students* so that the children can participate in ways comfortable to them."[25] Their study focused on and compared two teachers. It showed that the teacher who was willing to negotiate with students either the topic of discussion or the appropriate participation structure was better able to implement her lesson. Conversely, the teacher who attempted to impose both the topic of discussion and the appropriate interactional rules was frequently diverted because of conflicts with students over one or the other factor. Unfortunately, as mentioned earlier, the interpretation and practical applications of this body of research have utilized a restricted definition of culture, devoid of its dynamic, ideological, and political dimensions. Similarly, ideological tensions and antagonisms present in linguistic-minority language and literacy efforts are seldom discussed; issues such as teacher biases and racism, as well as students' antagonism and resistance, are rarely unmasked. Instead, teaching and learning difficulties are chiefly attributed to depoliticized notions of cultural differences.

Without identifying the ideological and political dimensions of culture and subsequent unequal status attributed to members of different ethnic groups, readers may conclude that teaching methods simply need to be ethnically and linguistically congruent to be effective; these readers may not recognize that not all ethnic and linguistic cultural groups are viewed and treated as equally legitimate in classrooms. Interestingly, there has been little discussion of the minority groups' historical and present-day subordinate status vis-à-vis white teachers and peers in these studies. All differences have been treated as ethnic cultural or linguistic differences and not as responses of teachers from dominant groups to low-status students and vice versa. It may be that educational problems have more to with asymmetry of power relations than with race, culture, or ethnicity per se.

Despite the fact that the cultural incongruence literature, for the most part, does not explicitly examine the effects of adverse race relations and notions of deficit on real or perceived cultural "differences," I believe that this body of work is undeniably useful in illustrating teacher strategies that consciously or unconsciously neutralize antagonistic teacher-student relations or teacher deficit ideology. These studies show the positive academic and social benefits that can result from teacher efforts to equalize relations by respecting and building on students' primary discourses. The teachers, in all of the studies discussed, learned about the students' primary discourses and learned to value them. In addition to learning about students' primary discourses, it is equally important to identify characteristics of the dominant culture's secondary discourses that need to be taught (in an additive fashion) to low-status students, who generally do not have access to highly valued discourses outside the classroom.

While recognizing that high social value in part reflects greater social and political realities, educators must tease out and identify those communication and language skills that result from dominant cultural practices that are rarely made explicit and taught to students from low-status cultural groups. Furthermore, in addition to identifying these skills, educators must implicitly and explicitly teach them so as to assist their students in critically acquiring the codes of the dominant class.

In the next section of this chapter, I discuss literature that specifically examines the linguistic contextualizing strategies of mainstream and nonmainstream students. This body of literature is expected to complete the understanding of the language and literacy practices of linguistic-minority students in school.

Cultural Differences in Student Use of Linguistically Contextualized Language

The studies mentioned in the following passages focused on the ability (and inability) of linguistic-minority students to contextualize their oral and written messages by relying chiefly on linguistic contextualizing conventions. As I have mentioned, the ability to contextualize utterances and text through primarily linguistic means rather than through less formal and academic ways is reported to be positively related to reading and writing achievement. In fact, some argue that although it is possible for young children to read low-level texts and write single words and short sentences, it is not possible to succeed in more advanced grades without the ability to produce and comprehend language that is linguistically contextualized.[26]

The studies reviewed in this section suggested that academically successful students are able to communicate using linguistically contextualized language.[27] The researchers in these studies analyzed the children's languages and then arbitrarily placed them along a continuum with two extremes: extralinguistically contextualized language (with a reliance on physical cues) and *de*-contextualized language (with a reliance on lexical and syntactic cues), which are placed on opposite poles.[28] However, it is important to point out that this model of two extremes is used purely as a heuristic since the assumption of "fully contextualized or fully *de*-contextualized language skills of course constitute only the endpoints (endpoints rarely encountered in real life) of an underlying continuum."[29] Although I problematize the notion of de-contextualized language both here and in Chapter 1, I use these categories and terminologies because they reflect the current paradigm of research, presented in this chapter.

As noted previously, a sociocultural view of language and literacy recognizes that "all adults control the basic cognitive functions. What differs are habitual ways of perceiving relationships and conventions governing how language is used."[30] However, this perspective in no way minimizes the importance of identifying communicative skills, no matter how culturally specific, that are necessary for academic success in schools. The selected research studies in this section illustrate the relationship of linguistically contextualized language with academic success.

Topic Organization Style

Sarah Michaels and John Collins's study investigated linguistically contextualized oral language use and its relationship to reading and writing achievement.[31] These researchers examined the oral discourse styles exhibited by working-class African American and middle-class white first-grade children during classroom sharing time. The study was conducted in order to better understand the speaking and writing problems that could result from students' reliance on extralinguistic contextualized language cues. The researchers analyzed children's language for thematic cohesion, which refers to the style by which a speaker or writer unifies a spoken or written text and includes linguistic devices to highlight certain information and background other information, as well as to signal topic shifts.

Michaels and Collins reported that during sharing time, the middle-class white children tended to use a "topic-chaining" communicative style understood by the teacher. This style consists of *explicitly* introducing one topic of conversation and elaborating on it. Conversely, the working-class African American children tended to use a style labeled "topic-associating." This style consists of a series of segments linked in what was perceived by the researchers as an *implicit* manner. Because the African American children's style of establishing theme was different from that expected by the teacher, the teacher often misunderstood the children's intent; she consistently interrupted them and erroneously asked them to stay on the subject.

The middle-class white children also employed a range of lexical and syntactic devices throughout their narratives; the working-class African American children, especially the girls, relied more heavily on prosodic cues, such as intonation and rhythm, to create a context. Michaels and Collins reported that different intonation patterns in working-class African American speech function much like lexical and syntactic cues in middle-class white speech. However, they can usually be understood correctly by members of the same cultural group because interpretation depends on familiarity with the culture-specific uses of intonation and prosody used to link text during conversation. Both styles, though communicatively effective, make different interpretational demands on the listener. The middle-class white children's talk required listeners to have mainstream middle-class knowledge of standard English lexicon and syntax; the African American children's talk required listeners to have specific African American cultural knowledge of the meanings of vowel elongation and contoured intonation.

During the second part of their experiment, Michaels and Collins examined how students organized topics in written narratives. Again, they reported that the working-class African American students' written texts were ambiguous and implicit precisely at those points where the children employed prosodic cues in their oral speech. Their conclusion was that children's spoken discourse styles have significant consequences for their acquisition of literacy, suggesting that certain conversational styles are more compatible with both oral and written linguistically contextualized language.

Exophoric and Endophoric Pronoun Use

Herbert Simons and Sandra Murphy also examined the discourse characteristics of working-class African American children and middle-class white children in their analysis of data from the School-Home Ethnography Project.[32] In their analysis, these authors focused on the students' use of exophoric and endophoric pronouns and their relationship to reading achievement.

An endophoric pronoun refers to an item previously mentioned in a text (for example, "the girl carried *the cheese to the boy* and gave *it* to *him*," where *it* is *the cheese* and *him* is *the boy*). An exophoric pronoun does not refer to an antecedent. Utterances with more exophoric pronouns are less explicit and usually depend on contextual information, such as intonation, to signal who or what the referent is (for example, "*he* saw *him* and *he* was mad," where it is unclear who *he* and *him* are). However, it is important to note that greater use of endophoric pronouns does not automatically render discourse more explicit; these pronouns must be placed either before or after the antecedent so as to avoid ambiguous or confusing references.

The investigators asked the subjects to describe some abstract figures in a way that would help a peer who was not present (an imaginary distant audience) to identify the figures. The children's speech was analyzed for exophoric and endophoric pronoun use. The proportion of endophoric language calculated per unit of language was found to correlate positively with reading achievement as measured by a California Test of Basic Skills reading subtest. The researchers reported that students who relied on linguistic cues to contextualize their language were generally better readers. Their findings suggest a positive relationship between linguistically contextualized language use and high achievement scores on standardized reading tests.

Exposure to "Book" Language

Another important study, conducted by Gordon Wells, examined the uses of language and literacy among low- and middle-socioeconomic-level families and children both in the home and at school over a ten-year period.[33] The sample was composed of native English-speakers. Wells reported that the best predictor of the child's early success in reading was exposure to storytelling. He stated that the extent of the children's own understanding of the purposes and mechanics of literacy at the time they started school was strongly associated with their exposure to this culturally valued practice. Although children tended to focus on meaning or content during storytelling, Wells maintained that listening to stories served to familiarize them with the form and structure of linguistically contextualized "book talk," as well as with some functions of reading.

Wells was less concerned with having students learn the mechanics of literacy than with the development of familiarity with the ways in which language is used in written discourse. He explained that, in general, children's difficulty with reading derives from reading's abstract nature—the locus of meaning in written text is within the text itself (linguistically contextualized), but the locus of meaning in speech is normally in the interaction between participants and in their shared knowledge (extralinguistically contextualized). Listening to stories provides children with the opportunity to learn some essentials of written language, as well as to extend and fictionalize experience. Reading and discussing stories helps children cope with the more linguistically contextualized spoken language the school curriculum demands.

Researchers consistently report the positive relationship between students' ability to comprehend and produce linguistically contextualized language and their reading and writing success. Advanced levels of reading and writing require students to comprehend and produce oral and written utterances that do not require extralinguistic or situational information in order to be explicit. The studies suggest that everyday communicative ability is not sufficient for the development of this particular language ability.

Formal and Informal Definitions

In their work with high-socioeconomic-status bilinguals, Catherine Snow and her associates examined the definitions of ten words offered by second- through fifth-grade students at the United Nations International School, a large private school in New York City that serves both international and U.S. upper-middle-class students.[34] They administered the Wechsler Intelligence Scale for Children (Revised) (WISC-R) vocabulary subtest and categorized students' responses as contextualized either formally or informally. Formal definitions were defined as containing an equivalency statement and some form of superordinate (for example, a donkey is an animal; a diamond is a thing), and informal definitions were defined as those lacking the equivalency statement and superordinate.

The authors of this study reported a positive relationship between the children's standardized test scores and their production of formal definitions on the vocabulary task. They mentioned that in a previous pilot study, the production of formal definitions also positively correlated with the students' tendency to revise written work and self-correct during oral picture description tasks. They concluded by emphasizing the need for further study of the students' use of linguistically contextualized language in the classroom in order to better understand the kinds of oral and written language that all students, especially second-language learners, need to develop for academic success.

Picture Description Tasks

Following Snow's methodology, Patricia Velasco and Ana María Rodino conducted similar studies with working-class Puerto Rican bilinguals in a northeastern public school system.[35] Velasco reported a similar relationship between the ability to linguistically contextualize language and English reading ability, as measured by standardized tests. Rodino's work demonstrated that working-class bilinguals were also capable of linguistically contextualizing picture descriptions when asked to do so for an imaginary distant audience. Interestingly, she reported that the children in her sample could linguistically contextualize more efficiently in English than in their native language, Spanish. Thus, she concluded that in her study, the bilingual students were experiencing attrition, or the loss of their Spanish-language skills.

The *de*-contextualized language research has begun to identify specific linguistic surface features that render linguistic messages overtly explicit and "appropriate" to classroom teachers. The majority of these studies have compared and contrasted the linguistic organizing styles and use of prosody of middle-class white and working-class African American students. Studies by Wells, Snow, Snow and associates, Velasco, and Rodino have provided additional information regarding the linguistic performance of middle- and working-class British students, high-socioeconomic-status bilinguals, and working-class mainland Puerto Rican bilingual students.[36]

The findings across studies strongly suggest that middle- and high-socioeconomic-status pupils come to school with knowledge about and an ability to utilize the types of linguistic cues and text-organizing styles expected in school contexts. The African American working-class students in the studies employed contextualizing cues described by the researchers as less academic and more dependent on extralinguistic situational and prosodic cues than on chiefly linguistic (lexical and syntactic) ones. Working-class mainland Puerto Rican students recognized contexts in which they were expected to speak and write in overtly explicit ways. They attempted to utilize linguistic cues but relied mainly on a greater use of adjectives (for example, colors of objects in the pictures described to imaginary distant audiences). They did not, however, modify sentence structure, and they did not utilize a greater number of adjectives that were more precise than colors, as did middle-class white students in the other studies.

Gee's concept of discourse is particularly useful in objectively understanding the *de*-contextualized language findings discussed here. More conventional views might see the nonwhite students' language use as deficient or culturally different and attribute the middle-class white children's academic success to their ability to learn the academic discourses of the dominant culture. However, I believe Gee's framework offers a more comprehensive explanation. Middle-class white children are simply privileged (through no effort of their own) because they come to school with a primary discourse (worldview, values, language uses, and so forth) that does not simply *resemble* the school discourse but actually represents a basic version of the discourse expected in schools. Although the discourses may not be identical, they share a basic ideological foundation.

Common perceptions suggest that middle-class white students experience a "better fit" in schools because they come from homes that promote literacy practice and skills that *coincidentally* match those taught in the schools. A conventional cultural mismatch or incongruence theory also focuses on the "better fit" that middle-class white students experience in school and attributes the phenomenon to cultural congruence. This theory stops short of highlighting the fact that educational institutions, like other institutions, reflect the dominant culture's ideology, values, and ways of using language and behaving.

Thus, instead of attributing the academic success of middle-class white students to cultural congruence and the academic underachievement and failure of nonwhite working-class students to cultural incongruence, Gee clearly illustrates that the primary discourses of a society's dominant cultural group and the secondary discourses valued by the greater society are not simply culturally congruent; rather, they are related discourses that grow out of one cultural group's ideological frameworks and preferred language and literacy practices. Members of nondominant or low-status cultural groups who attempt to acquire socially valued secondary discourses are attempting to gain membership in the dominant cultural group. But to become a member of this group, one must either be born into it or be apprenticed in it by someone familiar with the dominant culture.

The notion of discourses is useful for a better understanding of why middle-class white students appear to be sophisticated users of linguistic contextualizing cues even as their working-class nonwhite peers appear less proficient. The reasons for this discrepancy in performance are not solely cultural, for "it turns out (for historical, social and political reasons) that the [middle-class white child's] home-based Discourse is, while certainly different in various respects from school-based Discourses, more similar to many of them."[37]

Understanding the relationship between membership in dominant or subordinate groups and the acquisition of dominant secondary discourses has important implications for the teaching (or nonteaching) of dominant secondary discourses in school settings. In order for nonmembers to acquire socially valued language forms, such as linguistic contextualizing strategies, they must be willing to be apprenticed by a member of the dominant group who is willing to mentor a nonmember.

In the linguistically contextualized language studies reviewed, there was little discussion regarding why teachers in the classroom studies did not apprentice their linguistic-minority students into more academic ways of communicating. Despite the fact that she did not conduct a classroom study, Rodino articulated the urgent need for classroom teachers explicitly to teach their students to linguistically contextualize their utterances in formal academic settings.[38]

It is interesting that even though the majority of the teachers in the cultural incongruence classroom studies discussed earlier identified their students' language as not entirely appropriate, little was reported regarding teacher efforts to make explicit for students the language forms expected and considered appropriate in a classroom or to create learning situations in which the students could both learn and acquire linguistically contextualized ways of speaking and writing. The importance of linguistic *form* utilized in classroom contexts was highlighted in all the studies reviewed. Indeed, if teachers focused on content instead of form, many of the linguistic-minority students' utterances might have been judged as comprehensible and appropriate. However, the correctness of the form and not the meaning is usually focused on when there is some ideological benefit to be gained by stressing the surface features of the language, as Gee explained: "Unfortunately, however, many middle-class mainstream status-giving Discourses often *do* stress the surface features of the language. Why? Precisely because such surface features are the best test as to whether one was apprenticed in the 'right' place, at the 'right' time, and with the 'right' people."[39]

In fact, as many of the studies illustrated, teachers often unknowingly function as "gatekeepers" who focus on students' use of linguistic form over substance to sift the "right sort" of student out from the "wrong sort." Often, because their lack criticity and exposure to various and conflicting discourses, it is easy for teachers to become prescriptive in their expectations of students' language use and behavior in the classroom. Furthermore, the tendency seems to be to blame the students' homes, cultures, and socioeconomic status when the they do not already possess particular language skills.

In the studies in which linguistic-minority students did not possess mainstream, school-like ways of using language, very little beyond remediation efforts was discussed. Nothing was written questioning why teachers fail to apprentice and mentor precisely those students who do not already possess socially valued language and literacy abilities. The vestiges of a deficit orientation continue to be evident, and teachers fail to recognize that students' lack of familiarity with dominant discourses "does not mean . . . that the lack of these experiences develops in these children a different 'nature' that determines their absolute incompetence."[40]

In fact, although it may be extremely challenging for mainstream teachers to apprentice linguistic-minority students into dominant discourses, it is not impossible. Gee made two suggestions for effectively mentoring linguistic-minority students: (1) that teachers create classrooms that provide active apprenticeships in "academic" social practices and connect these social practices to real-life practices outside the classroom, and (2) that they teach "mushfake Discourse" because true and full acquisition of the secondary discourse by linguistic-minority students is probably not possible in many cases. The term *mushfake* is a term from prison culture meaning to make do with something less when the real thing is not available:

> [Mushfake Discourse means] partial acquisition coupled with meta-knowledge and strategies to "make do" (strategies ranging from always having a memo edited to ensure plural, possessive and third person "s" agreement errors to active use of Black culture skills at "psyching out" interviewers, or to strategies of "rising to the meta-level" in an interview so that the interviewer is thrown off stride by having the rules of the game implicitly referred to in the act of carrying them out).[41]

The solution, then, is that teachers teach mushfake strategies while teaching secondary dominant discourses to low-status students to ensure that they learn and acquire the discourse in order to become as fluent as possible.

There is a pressing need for research studies that examine the discourse apprenticeship process undertaken by mainstream teachers and linguistic-minority students. In particular, it is important to conduct linguistic studies in classrooms where the teachers perceive themselves to be cultural mentors and assume the role of advocates for their linguistic-minority students.

The majority of studies that examine children's contextualizing styles have focused on performance in the early elementary grades during storytelling and sharing events. Studies that include upper elementary students have limited their examinations of contextualizing styles to students' linguistic performance on language tasks specifically designed to elicit contextualizing strategies. There is a need to conduct classroom studies in upper elementary grades during academic discourse events that are deemed likely to elicit more formal and academic language use from students. Even more important would be a study of this type in classrooms where the teachers perceive themselves to be cultural, linguistic, and academic mentors for their students. However, in order to effectively mentor students, teachers must be able to minimize the antagonism that often informs and shapes the education of minority students. Only through a greater understanding of how factors related to race, culture, gender, ethnicity, class, and language converge to produce specific realities can teachers begin to help students navigate through the ideology that often boxifies them into one or more of these categories. Teachers also need to understand the relationship between such boxification and the lack of access to the academic discourse that is privileged by the very social order that created the need for boxification in the first place.

3 *A Potentially Ideal Classroom*

In selecting a classroom to study, I made every effort to select one in which there would be a minimal teacher bias toward the students' non-standard language and their active resistance to the her efforts to teach them more standard and mainstream ways of speaking and writing. In this chapter, I describe the participants (the classroom teacher and eight target students) and the context (a bilingual classroom) and explain how they came together to constitute a potentially ideal setting for examining academic discourse practices.[1] The purpose of this discussion is twofold. One purpose is to provide the reader with contextual information about the participants and the context in order to better understand the research findings reported in Chapters 4 and 5. The second purpose is to offer this contextual information as evidence of the ideal nature of the classroom setting in which the teacher declares her care and commitment to the students and the students (and their parents) report positive attitudes toward schooling in general and toward their teacher in particular.

The Classroom Teacher

Amy Cortland, the teacher selected for this study, is an experienced bilingual teacher who is highly proficient in English and Spanish and familiar with her school district's bilingual education program. An Anglo native English-speaker, Cortland was selected because she met four key selection criteria. She is: (1) highly proficient in Spanish, (2) familiar and comfortable with Mexican culture, (3) an experienced teacher who has taught school both in Mexico and the United States, and (4) committed to improving the academic and linguistic achievement of all her students. The selection of these key criteria was based on the need to conduct research in a potentially ideal or optimal setting. In such a setting, the teacher would likely assume a role as cultural mentor for her students and effectively instruct them, and the students would likely have ample opportunities to speak and write across a variety of academic discourse settings.

Cortland learned Spanish as a second language. Her fluent command of the language and extensive knowledge of Mexican culture result from her teaching experience in Mexican schools. Of her seven years teaching experience, three were completed in Sinaloa, Mexico. Cortland's U.S. teaching experience is limited to Chávez Elementary School. As a result of her training in bilingual education and her teaching experience in Mexico, Cortland feels well qualified in her role as a bilingual teacher.

Cortland's philosophy of education is multicultural, and she strongly supports a maintenance (versus the more common, transitional) bilingual education model in which bilingual students continue to receive instruction in their native language even after they become fluent in English.[2] As a proponent of bilingual education, Cortland reports that one of her goals is to assist her students in performing at grade level and to use English and Spanish in academic and "correct" (standard) ways. One of her key concerns is that her students speak nonstandard versions of English and Spanish. She hopes to help the children make the transition from "playground" English and Spanish to "academic" English and Spanish, and she utilizes James Cummins's concepts of BICs and CALPs to make her language goals clear.[3] As she explained to me:

> It's important to me that my students become completely bilingual and are able to express themselves in English and Spanish in ways that are correct and academic. Most of my students come from Spanish-speaking homes and have learned English as a second language but the English they speak is "playground" English; they speak an informal kind of English that is O.K. for talking to buddies but is not O.K. in a school setting. I take Jim Cummins' work seriously and believe that I need to teach CALPs to my students since they already come with BICs.

When asked how she goes about teaching cognitive academic language skills, she responded that she purposely creates "lessons and activities that put the students on the spot to speak and write in more formal and school-like ways." Cortland also mentioned that she reads quality literature to the children in an effort to model standard English and Spanish. During a significant part of the data-collection phase of this study, the teacher read the novel *The Witch of Blackbird Pond*, by Elizabeth George Speare, to the children on English days and various Spanish reading texts on Spanish days.

To accommodate the use of two languages in her academic schedule, Cortland follows an alternate-day bilingual program. Except for language arts, which is offered solely in English, all other academic subjects (for example, social studies and science) are taught in both English and Spanish. An alternate-day bilingual education program requires that instruction be offered in either English or Spanish on an alternate-day basis. For example, if Monday is designated an English day, then Monday's instruction is offered in English only, and instruction on Tuesday is provided entirely in Spanish. This sequence is followed throughout the school year so that both languages are used an equal portion of the time.

In addition to teaching standard academic discourse, Cortland reported that her role as teacher encompasses more than teaching responsibilities. During our many conversations, she explained that, in addition to being a teacher, she is also a member of the local Mexican American community (she resides in the community), as well as a friend and confidant to many of the parents of her students. She explained that one of her key responsibilities as a teacher of linguistic-minority students includes introducing them to "mainstream" culture and "mainstream" ways of doing things:

> I think that, as a member of the mainstream, I can share with my students tips on how to do things in order to succeed here and in the later grades. Since many of their parents are immigrants, they are expected to help their parents figure out the new society. I want to prepare them to be the very best that they can be and that includes maintaining Spanish. In my opinion, there is no reason why they should have to lose their Spanish in order to become fully proficient in English. Although the school district supports a transitional bilingual education program, I run a maintenance classroom.

Upon entering the classroom, any visitor can discern it is bilingual. A "Welcome/*Bienvenido*" poster is mounted on the inside of the door. The majority of the bulletin boards contain bilingual messages, such as "Reading is an Adventure/*La Lectura es una Adventura*," and the designation "Science Center/*Centro de Ciencias*" is posted over the class library. In addition, both the English and Spanish alphabets are displayed above the front blackboard. Many of the instructional charts are also bilingual (for example, there are teacher-made labels on a human respiratory system chart). Furthermore, the class library is well stocked with both English and Spanish books. In her attempt to provide her students with balanced reading materials, Cortland purchases most of the Spanish books and novels for the classroom during her regular visits to Mexico.

Cortland's commitment to her students, her view of herself as a cultural mentor, and her commitment to promoting more formal and academic uses of English and Spanish in her classroom constitute key elements in the creation of an optimal classroom setting in which to examine linguistic-minority students' academic discourse patterns. The teacher appeared, at all times, to be a serious and culturally sensitive individual who worked hard to promote her students' academic achievement, linguistic development, and biculturalism.

A School's Commitment to Linguistic-Minority Students

Cortland's commitment to maintenance bilingual education and her cultural sensitivity mirror her school's approach to teaching linguistic-minority students. I chose to study one classroom teacher and her students at Chávez Elementary School precisely because the school offers an exemplary bilingual program. This well-developed program is designed to address the academic and linguistic needs of students with a limited proficiency in English, and it clearly embodies the district's commitment to bilingual education.

During the school year covered in this study, Chávez Elementary provided kindergarten through fifth-grade (K–5) instruction to approximately 651 students. Of these, approximately 69 percent were minority children, and 31 percent were majority or mainstream children. Most of students with limited proficiency in English came from Spanish-speaking homes. The largest language groups included Spanish-speakers (78 percent), Vietnamese-speakers (7 percent), and Cambodian-speakers (5 percent). Smaller numbers of students spoke the following primary languages: Portuguese (3 percent), Cantonese (3 percent), Laotian (2 percent), and Chinese (1 percent).[4] Thus, the target students selected for observation came from the largest linguistic-minority group in the school.

The Bilingual Education Program at Chávez Elementary is considered part of the school's Specialty Enrichment Program. Unlike the bilingual education programs at other schools in the district, which are transitional, Chávez's bilingual program is now a maintenance program. As a result, bilingual instruction is currently available in grades K–5. In addition to servicing youngsters with limited proficiency in English, the program allows students who are fluent in English and English-monolingual students to learn Spanish as a second language. This feature in the school's bilingual program attracts majority students to the school.

The Classroom Student Body

Cortland's classroom was selected for this study because it clearly reflected the school's additive bilingual approach to working with linguistic-minority students. I purposely selected a *bilingual* classroom in Chávez Elementary School because I wanted to observe academic language use in a setting where the students could comfortably express themselves in either English or Spanish as they desired—to gauge if linguistically contextualized language use occurred in different ways in the two languages. Conducting the study in a bilingual classroom also provided a greater opportunity to observe target students' English and

Spanish language use during classroom lessons, when language use is expected to be more formal and academic.

I selected a fifth-grade classroom because, as I discuss in Chapter 1, oral and written language demands in the upper elementary grades are more likely to require that students produce linguistically contextualized language in both oral and written modes.[5] In fact, as mentioned earlier, it is precisely when language requirements become more linguistically contextualized that Mexican American students and other linguistic-minority students begin to fall behind in school.[6]

The student body in Cortland's classroom consisted of 33 students—16 boys and 17 girls. Five of the students were identified as Anglo, and 28 were Mexican American. Of the 28 Mexican American students, 11 were identified as having a limited proficiency in English, and 17 were classified as fluent in English. During the classroom language phase of the study, I examined the language patterns of the whole group. However, I selected 8 target students for the language task component of the study.

Profiles of the Target Students

What follows is a brief introduction to the eight target students focused on during the second phase of the research study. The target students included four students each from the higher- and lower-achieving ability groups (designated as such by their performance on standardized tests). The children identified as higher-achieving students were: Marissa Nava, Miguel Lara, Blanca Mariscal, and Evaristo Parra. The children identified as lower-achieving students were: Felice Villalpando, Oscar Loaíza, Raquel Ibarra, and Joey Elenes.

I selected the target students based on five criteria identified by current literature as key student characteristics and significantly related to academic and linguistic achievement. Specifically, I selected the eight students on the basis of (1) academic achievement (four of the highest-achieving students and four of the lowest-achieving according to standardized test scores), (2) teacher recommendation of students for participation, (3) having been schooled only in the United States, (4) English-proficient identification, and (5) coming from a working-class immigrant household.[7] The following individual profiles introduce individual students and provide information regarding each student's family and his or her academic and linguistic background.

Marissa Nava. Marissa was born in Tijuana, Baja California, Mexico, and came to the United States with her parents as a two-year-old infant. She attended Chávez Elementary School from kindergarten through fifth grade. Her original enrollment in 1981 classified her as having a limited proficiency in English. Marissa's records indicate that although she received Spanish reading readiness training in kindergarten, most of her instruction has been entirely in English, with specialized English as a second-language (ESL) instruction. In 1986, after four years of English-only instruction, she was reclassified as proficient in English, having scored equally high in both English and Spanish on the language proficiency test.

Marissa comes from a family of four, including her parents and an older brother. Both parents were born and reared in Mexico, although her father, because of his residence in a border town and early exposure to life in the United States, feels he had grown up on both sides of the border. Mr. and Mrs. Nava emigrated to the United States in 1978. Mr. Nava had worked at a variety of laborer jobs, such as doing body work and selling used-cars, and he was involved in establishing his own used-car dealership at the time of my study. Mrs. Nava had recently worked as a part-time lunch monitor at Chávez Elementary School, after serving for one year as a volunteer at the school. Mr. Nava speaks English, but his wife does not.

Marissa's parents do not perceive themselves as educated. Her father reported having received some schooling—approximately three years of elementary education—in Mexico. Mrs. Nava, an orphan, never attended school and can neither read nor write. She values the importance of a strong education and told the researcher: "*Una buena educación es muy importante, y yo quisiera que [Marissa] fuera al colegio. Ese es mi mayor deseo*" (A good education is very important, and I'd like for Marissa to go to college. That is my greatest wish). She has high expectations for her daughter and is very proud of the fact that Marissa translates and takes care of her correspondence for her.

Marissa was perceived by her fourth- and fifth-grade teachers as intelligent, motivated, and proficient in both English and Spanish, although she tended to code-switch quite frequently in conversations with peers. The teachers concurred that Marissa was a better reader and writer in English but that she continued to have difficulty with English vocabulary development. Her fourth-grade teacher described Marissa's oral English as "playground English" and her oral Spanish as "social Spanish" from the *ranchos* (rural areas). Cortland perceived Marissa as intelligent and a good reader and writer "if she can ever quiet down." Mrs. Nava described her daughter similarly and added that she was also quite rebellious and liked to challenge authority figures.

Miguel Lara. Miguel was also born in a border town—Ciudad Juárez, Chihuahua—and came to the United States with his parents at the age of one in 1977. He attended kindergarten in one school and grades 1 through 4 at another before arriving at Chávez Elementary. Miguel participated in a bilingual education program for three years. He was initially classified as not proficient in English and received native-language (Spanish) reading instruction in first and second grades. In third grade, he was reclassified as fluent in English and was transitioned to English-only instruction, until entering Cortland's bilingual fifth-grade classroom.

Miguel's family includes five people: himself, his parents, and two younger sisters. Mr. Lara had recently become co-owner of a photography shop; his wife both kept house and assisted him with the shop. Mr. and Mrs. Lara were born and educated in Mexico, where they both received their elementary and secondary educations. In addition, Mr. Lara took one year of public accounting courses, and Mrs. Lara had one year of secretarial training. Mr. Lara speaks and comprehends English; Mrs. Lara reports only receptive ability.

Both parents stress that it is important for Miguel to do well in school, and they hope that he will pursue a professional career in law or architecture. Mrs. Lara explained, *"Se le premia si saca buenos grados y se le castiga—una buena regañada, nunca se le pega—si no [saca buenos grados]"* (We reward him when he gets good grades and we punish him—we scold him, we don't hit him—if he doesn't [get good grades]).

The parents explained that they try to help Miguel with his homework when they can. In addition, they stress the use of Spanish in the home because they value maintaining the language. Even when Miguel attempts to speak to them in English, they pretend not to understand so that he will remember to speak Spanish to them.

Miguel was the most serious and reserved of the target students. Cortland reported that he was the type of student who did not like answering questions and preferred getting his work done with partners in small group settings. In addition, she described him as one of the most balanced bilingual students in the class. She perceived him to be the student most affirmative and proud of being Mexican and a Spanish-speaker. During Spanish instruction days, Miguel was one of the few students who responded to the teacher in Spanish. The teacher attributed his good grades to "brains, parental support, motivation, and early native language instruction."

Blanca Mariscal. Blanca was born in the United States to Mexican immigrant parents. In kindergarten, she was tested and classified as having a limited proficiency in English. Although she learned Spanish as her first language, Blanca arrived at school speaking some English and received English-only instruction from kindergarten through fourth grade. After one year of instruction, Blanca was reclassified as fluent in English.

Blanca comes from a family of eight: parents, five daughters, and one son. She is the youngest child. Both parents were born and reared in Mexico. Mr. Mariscal completed elementary school in Mexico and two years of English as a second language in El Paso, Texas. Mrs. Mariscal completed junior high school and a beauty-college course in Mexico. At the time of the study, her husband worked as a cook, and she was a housewife, although she also worked in a canning factory when work was available.

Mrs. Mariscal's attitude toward school seems quite positive. She perceives instructional methods as more sensitive to children and more child centered than in the past. Mrs. Mariscal believes that, although educational requirements are higher now, student preparation has improved and better prepares students to meet the higher requirements.

Mrs. Mariscal hopes that her daughter will enter a career but refused to state her career preference for her daughter because "*Ya no los puedo mandar—ellos tienen sus propio criterio*" (I can't order them about anymore—they have to make their own decisions).

Blanca is clearly English-dominant; she prefers speaking, reading, and writing in English. Blanca was talkative and outgoing in class with her peers. She was described by her mother and teacher as intelligent but slightly lazy and immature. Cortland reported that Blanca is a good reader and writer. She described her as a good comprehender and a creative writer who would probably get even better grades if she concentrated harder on her work and turned in assignments as scheduled. In addition, the teacher reported that although Blanca has only received one year of formal Spanish instruction, her oral/written receptive and production abilities in Spanish have increased significantly.

Evaristo Parra. Evaristo was born in northern California to a Mexican American mother and a Salvadoran father. His father emigrated to the United States in 1973, and Evaristo was born three years later. Evaristo's family has five members: Evaristo, his father, and three sisters. Like Blanca, Evaristo arrived in kindergarten speaking English, and his parents requested placement in an English-only classroom. However, it was not until 1984 (in third grade) that Evaristo was tested and reclassified as fluent in English. He attended four schools in a period of six years. In spite of his earlier status of having a limited proficiency in English, Evaristo was the least bilingual of the group. He was clearly dominant in English and felt stronger in that language, although he stated that he hoped to become more proficient in Spanish. Evaristo spoke English at school and with his siblings at home and both English and Spanish to his father.

Evaristo's parents divorced in 1983, and Evaristo and his sisters were divided among different relatives for approximately one year. The four children were eventually reunited with their father, and he currently has sole custody of the children. At the time of the study, Mr. Parra had left his job as a welder and was working as a refrigerator repairman. He had received an elementary and junior high education as well as training as a public accountant in El Salvador. Mr. Parra places a high value on schooling and feels that a good education is the only legacy he can leave his children, given his economic position. He said, "*La educación es muy necesaria y yo les he dado éso como meta y deseo que sobresalgan*" (An education is very necessary and I have given them that as a goal and I hope that they excel). He explained that because he worked, he was not able to visit the school, supervise his children's homework, or monitor the amount of television they watched. However, Mr. Parra believes that his children love and want to please him and would, therefore, do whatever is necessary to succeed in school.

Evaristo was described by Cortland as the most articulate and outwardly confident of the target students. He was well aware of his academic standing and his capacity to learn. The teacher added that he was also one of the few target students who enjoyed speaking in class and bidding for the teacher's attention, although he preferred to speak from his seat and not in front of the class.

Both his fourth- and fifth-grade teachers spoke very highly of Evaristo. They concurred that he is highly intelligent and has great potential. The fourth-grade teacher described him as "gifted" and reported that he had "a well-developed English vocabulary and wasn't afraid to use it." She also stated that he was very confident; even when he did not know a specific bit of information, he was always willing to take a guess. Cortland described him as a potential A+ student and blamed his average grades on his tendency to procrastinate.

Felice Villalpando. Felice was born in Dos Aguas, Michoacán, and arrived in the United States at two months of age. She is the sixth of eight siblings; she has two older married sisters, three older brothers, and two younger brothers. Felice received all of her schooling at Chávez Elementary, including two years of bilingual instruction. Her third-grade records indicate that she was transitioned to English-only instruction at the beginning of third grade. Interviews with her fourth-grade teacher confirmed that Felice's instruction in the third and fourth grades had been entirely in English.

Felice began her school career classified as having a limited proficiency in English, based on language proficiency scores. She was reclassified as fluent in English in 1984, after having been transitioned into an English-only classroom. Both her fourth- and fifth-grade teachers perceived her as being dominant in English, as well as preferring English over Spanish.

Mr. and Mrs. Villalpando have alternated between blue-collar employment and periods of unemployment. At the time of the study, Mr.

Villalpando was working as a janitor, and Mrs. Villalpando was temporarily disabled from an accident she had suffered on the job at a cannery. Neither parent had received more than a fourth-grade education in Mexico. Mrs. Villalpando reported: "*Estudié muy poco—hasta cuarto or quinto porque ya no hubo maestro, Viviamos a la orilla del pueblo*" (I studied very little—up to fourth or fifth grade because there was no teacher to teach us. We lived on the outskirts of town).

Mr. Villalpando explained that he received little schooling because he had helped his father work their land; the schooling he received had not been much help. The Villalpandos did not consider themselves to be proficient in English.

Both parents feel unable to help Felice with her schoolwork and expect the older siblings to assist each other. In addition, Felice's mother often buys books on sale and has purchased a series ranging from religious paraphernalia to computer catalogs. However, Mrs. Villalpando worries that Felice will forget Spanish because "*es mejor saber los dos idiomas, pero el español no le gusta*" (it's much better to know both languages, but she doesn't care for Spanish).

Felice was one of the most serious children in the study. Boys often sought her out to joke with her and tease her, and she responded by ignoring them; most of the other girls would join in the kidding. Both her fourth- and fifth-grade teachers commented on her serious attitude toward school. Although they both rated her reading and writing ability as "average" to "slightly below average," they perceived her as hardworking and anxious to please her teachers. Ms. Cortines, the fourth-grade teacher, described Felice as "'a doll' who always wanted to do the job right," and Cortland described her as "a perfectionist, a goody-two-shoes." Mrs. Villalpando also commented on her daughter's love of school and reading: "*Hay veces que la mando a dormir y se queda dormida con los libros encima*" (There are times when I send her to bed and she falls asleep with her books on top of her).

Oscar Loaíza.   Oscar was born in San José, California, to a Mexican American mother and a Puerto Rican father. Oscar had attended Chávez Elementary School since his enrollment in kindergarten in 1981. He was classified as having a limited proficiency in English at that time but was reclassified as fluent in English in first grade. Oscar entered school speaking some English because his mother is fully bilingual. The student received two years of bilingual instruction in the course of his elementary education.

Oscar comes from a small family; his only sibling is a younger brother. Both parents speak English. Mrs. Loaíza considers herself equally bilingual, although she prefers to speak Spanish with her family at home. Oscar's mother completed nine years of education in the United States. Mr. Loaíza attended school through the second grade in Puerto Rico and reported being able to read and write in Spanish, although not as proficiently as he would prefer. He is currently disabled but previously worked as a janitor. Mrs. Loaíza works as a school aide at Chávez Elementary. She assists in the cafeteria and with yard duty during recess and lunch periods.

Mrs. Loaíza describes her son as very intelligent but just a bit lazy. However, she perceives him as doing well in school and reports no difficulty with schoolwork. She explained that when Oscar is interested in a topic, he does well in school. Mrs. Loaíza values education and regrets not going further herself. She hopes Oscar will go to college and that he will apply himself in school. "*Siempre le digo, 'Lo único que puedo darles es una educación y es muy importante, especialmente ahora que está tan cara la vida. El estudio es muy valioso'*" (I always tell him, "The only thing I can give you is an education, and it is very important, especially now that the cost of living is so expensive. School is very valuable").

Oscar is a talkative and fun-loving boy. He was the most sociable and verbal of the boys in the sample. Oscar also seemed to be one of the most popular boys in the classroom; he was always surrounded by and interacting with his peers. Cortland described Oscar as bright but undisciplined. She added that Oscar could probably do better in school if he would concentrate more on his work than on socializing. Oscar is English-dominant and achieves better in academic subjects presented in English. The classroom teacher described Oscar as an extreme extrovert who enjoys talking and sharing in class as well as socializing with his peers. She attributed his below-average academic standing to immaturity and to his unclear perceptions of his own skills. Because of these attributes, Oscar experiences confusion when he receives poor grades.

Raquel Ibarra.   Raquel arrived in the United States at three years of age, with her parents and one younger brother. She attended three other schools (including preschool) in the Los Angeles area prior to entering the third grade at Chávez Elementary School. Raquel was classified as having a limited proficiency in English upon entering Chávez Elementary and was reclassified as fluent in English in 1986 (in fourth grade).

Raquel comes from a single-parent household. Her mother and father are divorced. Mr. Ibarra is employed as a machinist in Los Angeles, and Mrs. Ibarra is employed in a local factory as a label-maker. Both parents were born in Mexico and received their primary education there. Mrs. Ibarra completed five years of elementary education. She was unable to provide information regarding Mr. Ibarra's years of schooling. At the time of the interview, Mrs. Ibarra described herself as limited in English.

Mrs. Ibarra perceives her daughter as a shy and sweet child who experiences difficulty in school because she has problems understanding academic instruction. Mrs. Ibarra believes her daughter is intelligent but requires one-on-one instruction. She feels that her daughter is hardworking but requires more time and attention than is usually allowed in school in order to complete her academic tasks successfully. Mrs. Ibarra hopes that Raquel will finish high school and join the army to learn a career because she anticipates not being able to afford a college education for her daughter.

At the time of the study, Raquel read and wrote English at a high-second-grade/low-third-grade level. Cortland explained that Raquel performed much better on English tasks than on Spanish ones. Both her mother and her teacher reported that she preferred reading romance novels and writing poetry and love letters to engaging in academic reading and writing tasks. Raquel's fourth-grade teacher described the student as a "dreamer" and a "socializer" who had difficulty concentrating on schoolwork. Raquel does not perceive herself as a good reader or writer. She attributes her difficulty to being unable to pronounce (decode) words whose meanings she knows. She also considers herself stronger in English but expressed a desire to become more proficient in Spanish because "it's better to know two languages than just one." However, she prefers English to Spanish because it is "easier" and because it will help her with a career. In spite of her difficulties in school, Raquel wants to attend college to become a nurse or a teacher.

Joey Elenes.   Joey was born in San Francisco, California, of Mexican parents. He attended three schools before Chávez Elementary. Joey was initially classified as having a limited proficiency in English in 1983 and reclassified as fluent in English in 1985 (in third grade). All of Joey's education prior to the fifth grade was provided in English-only classrooms. Mrs. Elenes explained that in spite of her son's initial limited-English status, she requested English-only instruction because she wanted her son to learn English as quickly as possible. She now believes she may have made a mistake and that Joey would have benefited greatly from native-language (Spanish) instruction in a bilingual classroom.

Joey comes from a small family, consisting of himself, his father, his mother, and a younger brother. Both parents were raised in the state of Guanajuato, Mexico. Mrs. Elenes was born in Mexico. Mr. Elenes was born in Alhambra, California, but grew up in Mexico. At the age of thirteen, he returned to California to seek employment. He completed three years of elementary schooling in Mexico, and Mrs. Elenes completed four years.

Both parents report some receptive English ability but little speaking ability. Mr. Elenes is currently disabled after twenty years of working as a janitor for a railroad company. Mrs. Elenes is a homemaker employed as a sorter for a local nut company whenever work is available.

In spite of both parents' limited education, Mrs. Elenes has always taken a keen interest in her son's education. She explains that she and her husband are unable to help their sons with their homework because of their limited English proficiency and education. Because of their limitations, they tend to focus on the neatness and completeness of Joey's homework assignments. Both parents value education and hope their sons will succeed and go to college. "*Quisiera que por lo menos estudiará unos tres años de colegio. Yo trabajaría el primer año para ayudarle, y luego él podría encontrarse un trabajo para ayudarse*" (I would like that he at least study three years of college. I could work the first year to help him, and then he could probably find a job in order to work his way through college).

Both parents hope that Joey can pursue studies to become a doctor or an electronics engineer so he will not have to exist as a "work mule," as they have had to do. (The Eleneses are not aware of how many years of study are necessary to achieve such career goals.)

Both Cortland and Joey's fourth-grade teacher attested to Mrs. Elenes's interest in Joey's academic achievement. She has a history of visiting the school often and participating in open-house meetings and other school events. Joey's fourth-grade teacher added that Mrs. Elenes attended a PTA-sponsored parent workshop every night for two weeks in spite of overall poor parent attendance.

Cortland described Joey as quite bright but shy and unwilling to speak in class. During the study, Joey was a quiet student; he only occasionally volunteered information in class, but he enjoyed asking questions during teacher and peer presentations. He reads and writes at the third-grade level and demonstrates a marked preference for English, both in the classroom and at home. Mrs. Elenes complains that he refuses to speak Spanish to his parents and demands that they speak English to him because "we're in America, not in Mexico."

Joey perceives himself as a good and fast reader who prefers comic books and "funnies" to school books. In addition, contrary to parent and teacher perceptions, Joey claims to value learning Spanish as much as learning English. He explains that knowing two languages will be helpful later in life when seeking employment.

It is evident from the discussion of individual portraits that there are a number of similarities in the target students' backgrounds. For example, equal numbers from both achievement groups were foreign- and U.S.-born. Family size was also similar across achievement groups. The mean family size was 5.4 members. In addition, the majority of the students (75 percent) came from homes that included both parents. Review of parent occupation indicated the majority of parents were employed in the blue-collar sector.

Although the background and demographic similarities are interesting in and of themselves, it is important to highlight comparisons that are related to the language and literacy focus of this study. What I found to be particularly striking about the student profiles is that, regardless of academic standing as defined by standardized test scores (and the parents were not familiar with most of these), all of the parents viewed the school's preparation of their children positively and with great hope. Although some (the parents of Oscar Loaíza, Raquel Ibarra, and Blanca Mariscal) acknowledged that their children could benefit from developing greater self-discipline and a drive to succeed, most parents viewed schooling as an extremely positive force in their children's lives. Over and over, they shared their belief that the only legacy they could leave their children, given their limited economic resources, was the opportunity to attend U.S. schools so they could improve their lot in life. The parents exhibited almost a blind faith that the public schools could and would transmit all of the social and academic capital needed by their children in order to succeed in later grades and in their adult lives in the United States.

Many of the parents felt frustrated with their inability to help their children with schoolwork. For example, Joey Elenes's parents reported doing the best they could, often focusing on the neatness of Joey's work and relying on his translations of homework requirements in order to try make sense of and assist him with his school assignments. Clearly, they had the best intentions but did not possess the appropriate cultural capital to help their child in navigating school culture and dealing with academic work. Given their own limited schooling, they viewed their duties as primarily related to imparting Christian values, an ethos of hard work, and a positive attitude toward school. In addition, many parents explained that though they could not intellectually nourish their children, they would nourish them in other ways. The mothers, for instance, reported working very hard to provide their children with healthy foods and a healthy life. During one informal conversation, Mrs. Loaíza informed me that she carefully planned meals at home to ensure that Oscar received the nutrition necessary for a growing boy. Similarly, Mrs. Lara and Mrs. Mariscal explained to me the importance of feeding the children fresh fruit and vegetables daily. Mrs. Villalpando focused on the need to provide children with regular exercise and fresh air and informed me of her family's regular weekend trips to the park.

The more highly educated parents, such as Mr. Parra and Mr. and Mrs. Lara, felt a bit more comfortable helping their children with schoolwork, but they still believed that academics were the responsibility of the school. Their chief responsibility was to ensure that their children were ready both physically and mentally to take advantage of the academic instruction imparted in the schools.

It was evident from my many informal discussions with the parents that they viewed their children as primed for taking full advantage of the academic and linguistic preparation provided by their teachers. They perceived their children as possessing the necessary attitudes, innate ability, and predisposition for learning. As far as the parents were concerned, all their children required was a teacher to impart the necessary academic and linguistic skills needed to succeed in the fifth grade and, it was hoped, beyond.

The parents' respect for Cortland and their faith in her ability to prepare their children academically was tremendous. Most of them perceived their children to be achieving at or close to grade level, and they did not mention any serious concerns about their children's academic performance or future success. This combination of faith in Cortland and their expectations of her is particularly relevant to my interest in learning if and how working-class linguistic-minority children in her classroom acquire academic discourse and linguistically contextualized language skills. Following the parents' line of reasoning, one can assume that the parents expect the teacher to teach their children the necessary language skills—including linguistic contextualizing language skills—to succeed in school. Educators need to completely understand that, as far as these parents are concerned, they send their children to school well nourished, healthy, and ready to learn. In other words, the parents believe that they have done their job and that teachers must do theirs.

4 The Misteaching of Academic Discourses: Three Discourse Events

In this chapter, I discuss the academic discourse used by students and by Amy Cortland, their teacher, in one fifth-grade English and Spanish bilingual classroom. Specifically, I examine Cortland's efforts to create participation structures that elicit students' production of linguistically contextualized language. I analyze, in particular, the students' ability to contextualize language mainly using linguistic contextualizing cues rather than less formal extralinguistic cues in the classroom during normally occurring lessons.

In the classroom, I examine student discourse for contextualizing cues used in the classroom during two commonly occurring language lessons. I also analyze the teacher's efforts to elicit linguistically contextualized cues from her students, as well as her responses to students' actual efforts. By examining the contextualizing cues used by bilingual Mexican American students during naturally occurring language events in the classroom, the ways in which the teacher implicitly or explicitly teaches and evaluates students' contextualizing strategies become evident. This dual focus on student and teacher language use required that I also examine teacher demands for and evaluations of students' contextualizing strategies.

The classroom language findings are surprising, given that my research took place in the well-organized bilingual classroom of an exemplary teacher. I describe the findings because, despite the teacher's conscious efforts to create classroom situations that would encourage students to use more formal and academic ways of speaking and writing, other factors tacitly short-circuited her efforts. The subversion was so successful that even the teacher, despite her articulated linguistic and academic goals, collaborated in transforming those situations into less formal ones, which, at times, were playful in tone. Under these circumstances, it was difficult to discern whether students *could not* linguistically contextualize their utterances or whether they simply *did not need to*, given the informal nature of the lessons.

What became clear and fundamentally important is that the teacher-student language disjunction created the potential for linguistic conflict. This potential exists in any classroom situation in which teachers attempt to impose or require a language variety not normally used by their students. Thus, teachers in English-only classrooms as well as their colleagues in bilingual classrooms (where English and a language other than English are used) need to be cognizant of this potential for conflict and student resistance when they teach in standard varieties of English or Spanish. The reality that significant numbers of linguistic-minority students (including those having a limited proficiency in English) are also present in mainstream English-only settings, often joining English-dominant peers who speak nonstandard English language varieties, makes it particularly urgent that both bilingual and English-monolingual educators critically understand the potential for linguistic conflict in the classroom and take steps to mediate it.

Research in bilingual and linguistic-minority education has not thoroughly addressed the issue of linguistic conflict, although some efforts have been made to explain the resistance of linguistic-minority students to learning a second language and culture.[1] Much of the literature continues to treat the phenomena of English as a second-language acquisition and acquisition of standard dialects as an apolitical undertaking that is relatively easy if students are cognitively capable language learners. Little empirical work examines the forms that linguistic conflict and student resistance take in classrooms where working-class students are expected to acquire standard varieties of English as well as the corresponding standard for their native language.

The Misteaching of Academic Discourses

Through the course of data analysis, a number of discourse patterns emerged in that I identified three frequently occurring discourse events with the potential to elicit linguistically contextualized language: (1) oral vocabulary and definition lessons; (2) oral presentations of written texts, described as events with the potential to elicit linguistically contextualized oral and written language from the students; and (3) solitary writing activities.

However, despite Cortland's conscious efforts to create classroom discourse situations that would elicit student use of more formal and academic ways of speaking, students' efforts to transform the discourse events into more informal and playful events short-circuited the teacher's pedagogy. The students' resistance to using the academic discourse was so successful that even the teacher, despite her articulated linguistic and academic goals, opted to support linguistic and cultural solidarity with her students rather than maintain her identified plan to teach and require student use of more formal academic discourse. For example, despite Cortland's efforts to create formal public-speaking situations in the classroom (as when she rearranged the classroom to simulate a formal auditorium setting and asked individual students to present at the front of the class), students indirectly refused to assume more formal roles as speakers. Instead, they turned the public-speaking event into a sort of comedy show in which the focus was on the comedic interaction between the speaker and members of the audience.

Such examples dramatically capture the inability of one well-intentioned and hardworking teacher to negotiate with her students both cultural solidarity and the use of more formal types of academic discourses, which necessarily require that speaker and audience assume a position of distance and disconnection. That is, when Cortland created learning contexts that required students to respond in less spontaneous and informal ways and utilize more formal discourse structures to convey an oral message, the students modified the learning contexts in order to render them less formal and distancing. Thus, the playful discourse that they produced ultimately "matched" the newly modified discourse event. Because of the value the teacher placed on maintaining solidarity with her students, she accepted the modifications of the learning contexts and the resulting student discourse, which reproduced the students' discourse behavior patterns as the dominant medium of communication in the classroom. Although Cortland would often privately voice her concerns to me that she did not understand why her Mexican American students were not able to produce more formal and academic discourse in either English or Spanish even though her Mexican students in Mexico (who were middle-class and schooled in private schools) could, she did not explicitly share her concerns with her students. The teacher's inability to understand class distinctions paralyzed her pedagogical options in addressing specific linguistic needs. Her concerns that students were not able to produce a more formal and academic discourse shifted the blame to the students' "inability" and away from her own pedagogy. Cortland was a well-intended and most dedicated teacher, but in the end, she appeared to be entrapped by a more deep-seated deficit orientation that points to nature as the cause of students' failure to produce more formal academic discourse.

During the lessons, Cortland proceeded to accept as correct the responses that the students produced, however unclear and brief, thereby creating a form of linguistic laissez-faire in her classroom. She often implicitly modeled the type of academic discourse that she hoped the students would eventually display, but she did not make her expectations explicit. Under these circumstances, it was difficult to discern whether students could not linguistically contextualize their utterances or whether they simply did not need to since the teaching of the academic discourse as the object of knowledge was relegated to the margins of the lessons so that the teacher could maintain linguistic and cultural solidarity with her students.

Common Academic Discourse Events

During my observations, I identified three discourse events (oral vocabulary and definition lessons, oral presentations of written text activities, and solitary writing tasks) based on the frequency of their occurrence as well as the likelihood that they would encourage student production of linguistically contextualized language strategies. All three types of events shared or contained social interactions that could have plausibly required the presenter to address a real or imaginary distant audience (teacher and/or peers), potentially assume little knowledge shared with the audience, and perceive the need to elaborate linguistic messages explicitly and precisely to minimize audience misinterpretation.

Throughout the discourse events, the focus of analysis alternated from student language use (the student as speaker and writer) to audience demands (teacher and peer demands and feedback). The demands of a distant audience potentially create a sociolinguistic situation in which students must not only behave in socially proper ways but also display the appropriate language skills—such as linguistically contextualized language—necessary to meet the specific linguistic demands of the social situation.[2]

The need to respond to a distant rather than an immediate audience potentially presents students with language use situations that are likely to encourage them to produce full and overtly explicit messages rather than partial and less overtly explicit ones. Audience support (immediacy) or lack of support (distance) can be gauged by the types of demands made by and the questions asked by the audience.

The focus on language production patterns across the three discourse events I examined dealt with student language and audience demands and feedback either simultaneously or alternately from student to audience. For example, during the vocabulary and definition language activities, I examined both teacher and student language use patterns. However, during oral presentations of written text, my attention shifted to the role the audience played in eliciting linguistically contextualized language from the students. Conversely, in the analysis of written text, I concentrated only on the students' language production and examined their use of linguistically contextualized written language strategies. The purpose of this shifting focus was to study the role of the audience as it affected (encouraged or discouraged) the students' production of linguistically contextualized language cues during their presentations of information.

Oral Vocabulary and Definition Lessons

Oral vocabulary and definition lessons required that students exhibit their understanding of word meanings. According to Catherine Snow, classroom teachers often distinguish between (1) student definitions that convey understanding of word meaning, and (2) the proper academic exhibition of definition strategies.[3] Discourse events such as the oral vocabulary and definition language activities were selected because the context in which they occurred was deemed likely to encourage students to exhibit knowledge to an audience (the teacher) who would probably provide little assistance and behave as a distant audience.

The oral vocabulary and definition discourse event met the three criteria for selection. First, it had the potential to encourage the student to address orally an imaginary distant audience that could provide little or no interactive help in conveying the meaning of definitions. Second, during this type of discourse event, the student was likely to have little or no encouragement to assume shared knowledge with the imaginary distant audience. Third, it was expected that during definition lessons, the students would perceive the need to elaborate linguistic messages precisely and explicitly to minimize misinterpretation.

In addition, oral vocabulary and definition discourse events occurred quite frequently across subject areas (for example, in reading, social studies, and science). Reading lessons were conducted entirely in English, and social studies, science, and language arts lessons were conducted in English and Spanish alternately. This type of language activity occurred across grouping situations and academic subjects. Thus, students defined vocabulary words in dyads, in whole groups, and in small-group settings. Approximately 61 percent of all classroom transcripts I analyzed centered on or contained one of these discourse events.

The purpose of the definition discourse event was to have the students orally demonstrate to their teacher their understanding of the word or phrase being defined. At times, the students displayed their knowledge in a verbal activity following up on an earlier written task (such as defining spelling words or completing vocabulary worksheets). Normally, however, the task was initiated in the oral mode. During these lessons, students were expected to display their knowledge of vocabulary words. Usually, the teacher compiled vocabulary lists from reading basals, workbooks, history books, and other classroom texts and reviewed them orally with the students.

The focus of this analysis centered on vocabulary and definition activities during which the teacher evaluated the students' definitions. A simultaneous focus on teacher and student language use was necessary to understand the role of the teacher as audience and to gauge more accurately student language production under formal academic conditions.

Discourse interaction patterns during oral definition discourse events followed a traditional initiation-response-evaluation (IRE) sequence. [4] The teacher's collaborative style usually allowed the students more than one opportunity to answer correctly and to receive a positive evaluation.

The discussion of language use during the IRE interaction sequence in this type of discourse event focuses on both student and teacher language production patterns. These language patterns are discussed under teacher initiation strategies, student response patterns, and teacher evaluation patterns in the following sections.

Teacher Initiation Strategies.   The initiation strategy most frequently employed by the teacher consisted of providing an unfinished sentence for the student to complete (for example, "When a worm becomes a butterfly, it is said to have undergone . . .). The second common teacher initiation strategy consisted of saying the vocabulary word without explicitly asking the student to define it (for example, "OK, metamorphosis"). Less preferred initiation strategies included asking, "What is [vocabulary word]?"; providing a complete sentence as a hint; providing other hints; and asking the students to use the vocabulary word in a sentence.

Approximately 37 percent of the teacher initiations consisted of unfinished sentences, and 21 percent were solitary vocabulary word presentations. The less preferred strategies—asking, "What is it?"; asking for a sentence with the word in it; and offering hints—were employed approximately 11 percent of the time. These preferred teacher initiation patterns suggest that the role of the teacher as audience in this type of language activity is supportive and helpful. The following questions and answers are illustrative (translations are italicized):

> TEACHER: Un "reino." No es lo mismo que un rey. El rey es una persona y su reino es su . . . (no student response). ¿Qué es un reino?
> STUDENT: ¿Tierra del rey?

TEACHER: Tierra del rey. Muy bien.

TEACHER: *A "kingdom." It is not the same as a king. A king is a person and his kingdom is his . . . (no student response). What is a kingdom?*

STUDENT: *The king's land?*

TEACHER: *The king's land. Very good.*

TEACHER: Palacio, ¿quién vive en el palacio?

STUDENT: El rey.

TEACHER: Ajá, ¿y un palacio es qué? Es un árbol, un mar . . . ¿es qué?

STUDENT:(response unintelligible)

TEACHER: ¿El rey vive en su . . . ?

STUDENT: Casa.

TEACHER: OK, un palacio es la casa del rey.

TEACHER: *Palace, who lives in a palace?*

STUDENT: *The king.*

TEACHER: *Umhum, and the palace is what? Is it a tree, an ocean is what?*

STUDENT: *(response unintelligible)*

TEACHER: *The king lives in his . . . ?*

STUDENT: *House.*

TEACHER: *OK, a palace is the king's home.*

Across oral vocabulary and definitions, the teacher consistently provided the students with meaningful contexts and hints to assist and encourage them to respond. She proved to be an extremely collaborative audience. Contrary to my expectations, the teacher did not distance herself from the students and demand that they think through their definitions in order to produce complete and overtly explicit definitions.

Student Response Patterns.   The teacher's collaborative role affected student responses in two ways: in the length of utterance and in the type of response. The students produced brief utterances and relied primarily on the use of synonyms, examples, and explanations to exhibit their knowledge of word meanings. Definition strategies such as these are contextualized and assume shared knowledge with the listener.[5]

Student responses averaged 3.11 words per utterance on the first set of responses and 5.72 words on the second set. Conversely, teacher evaluations and responses averaged 10.49 words per utterance on the first set of evaluations and 10.51 words on the second.

It is likely that student response patterns were affected by the teacher's solicitous initiations. It is also possible that the students did not feel the need to produce more explicit and formal definitions because the teacher assumed responsibility herself for providing the context as well as clarifying ambiguities, rather than requiring the students to do so. In addition, despite the brevity and implicitly contextualized nature of the students' responses, the teacher proved quite willing to accept them as appropriate.

This phenomenon is consistent with much of the literature on teacher and student classroom language; teachers typically dominate classroom discourse.[6] However, it is also likely that, given the teacher's solicitous approach, such brief student responses constituted academically, socially, and linguistically appropriate responses, as exemplified in the following questions and answers (translations are italicized):

TEACHER: "Prodigiosa," ¿alguien sabe lo que significa "prodigiosa"?
STUDENT: ¿Trabajador?
TEACHER: No, "prodigiosa" significa algo distinto. ¿Quién sabe? Por ejemplo, Tomás Jefferson fue una persona prodigiosa.
STUDENT: ¿Sabio?
Teacher: Era un sabio. Tenía muchos conocimientos y talentos. Era un sabio.
TEACHER: *"Prodigious," does someone know the meaning of "prodigious"?*
STUDENT: *Hardworking?*
TEACHER: *No, "prodigious" means something different. Who knows? For example, Thomas Jefferson was a prodigious person.*
STUDENT: *A scholar?*
TEACHER: *He was a scholar. He possessed a lot knowledge and talents. He was a scholar.*

It also appears that the teacher's extremely collaborative approach affected the *types* of definition strategies students employed. Because the teacher often provided the context or appeared willing to assume a shared background with the students, the students consistently utilized three definitional strategies: synonyms, examples, and explanations (identified in the literature as "contextualized")[7]. In the first set of student responses, 33 percent of the definition strategies contained synonyms, 15 percent examples, 8 percent explanations, 8 percent language switches, 3 percent formal definitions, 15 percent no responses, and 18 percent "other" responses.

In situations in which the teacher allowed the students a second opportunity to respond correctly, I observed similar definition strategies. Twenty-one percent of the definitions contained synonyms and examples, and 17 percent contained explanations. In addition, 13 percent were formal definitions, 8 percent language switches, 4 percent no responses, and 17 percent "other" responses. In summary, the students' preferred definition strategies were informal and not overtly explicit. Again, in spite of their informal nature, these strategies appeared appropriate given the task and the teacher's tendency to accept and evaluate them as correct.

Teacher Evaluation Patterns. The analysis of teacher evaluations corroborates the teacher's perceived appropriateness of student definitions. In response to the students' definitions, the teacher generally responded by accepting the responses. If the teacher was not entirely satisfied with the student definition, she often responded by providing additional hints or by giving the correct response herself. She seldom responded by requesting clarification or by offering a negative evaluation. Nonacceptance of student responses was accomplished in an indirect manner, such as when she provided the response herself or when she continued to probe for the correct response. In addition, the teacher offered assistance to improve the chances for a more appropriate response the second time around.

In the first set of evaluations, 28 percent showed acceptance of students' responses, 26 percent offered additional hints, and 23 percent provided the correct responses. In addition, 13 percent requested clarification, 5 percent corrected the students' response, and 5 percent consisted of "other" evaluations. The following examples illustrate the teacher's tendency to accept student responses without further probing and to provide students with a correct response.

> TEACHER: "Pollination," what is "pollination"?
> STUDENT: It's where the bees come and they get the stuff from the
>   flowers, the yellow stuff from the pollen.
> TEACHER: Good! Write that down.

> TEACHER: "Conspire." One [sentence] with "conspire." To talk softly
>   is to do what? What does it mean?
> STUDENT: You're going to do something bad.
> Teacher: OK, to make plans when you're going to do something
>   bad. What kind of people conspire?
> STUDENT: Thieves.
> TEACHER: Robbers, criminals. Who would like to make a sentence?
>   What you need to have is so and so conspire to do da-da-da.
>   They talk together and plan. The people conspire to kill.
> STUDENT: The people conspire to kill.
> TEACHER: Yes, good.

The interaction between teacher and student also shows that when the teacher allowed the student a second opportunity to respond, her evaluations of the response followed similar patterns. Fifty-two percent demonstrated acceptance of student responses, 24 percent consisted of providing hints, and 24 percent provided correct responses. The teacher was quite consistent in her role as audience. As with her initiation style, she was a most collaborative and accepting audience.

The primary language finding is that the oral vocabulary and definition activities did not constitute linguistically demanding discourse events for the students involved, even though they had the potential to do so. The teacher, in her role as audience, proved extremely supportive, as demonstrated by her consistent attempts to assist the students. By creating a language situation in which the students did not perceive the need to produce elaborate and overtly explicit definitions, however, the teacher, in effect, encouraged the production of informal language, counter to her role requiring her to teach the academic discourse. In fact, the teacher consistently treated the student responses as appropriate even when they were not. In my view, this not only is a form of misteaching but may also constitute a paternalistic attitude that results in de-skilling the students. Under these conditions, it was most likely that the students received the message that their responses were entirely adequate. What is at play in this teaching context is the teacher's need (perhaps unconscious) to develop a form of cultural solidarity with her students, a solidarity that, in the end, could result in the social promotion of students even though they have not demonstrated mastery of academic discourse skills deemed desirable by the teacher. The teacher's sabotage of her own explicit academic discourse teaching goals suggests her lack of understanding concerning the complexity and tensions present in the teaching of academic discourse to students who may be somewhat insecure in their own language and whose culture is often devalued by the dominant society. Furthermore, it denudes her deficit orientation ideology. In other words, by not recognizing her complicity in not teaching what she purportedly states in her goals, she displaces her own responsibility by blaming the students' inability to fully demonstrate their mastery of the targeted academic discourse skills.

The second discourse situation studied involved student oral presentations of written text. These presentations yielded similar results regarding the collaborative nature of the audience and the appropriateness of student assumptions of knowledge shared with interlocutors.

Student Oral Presentations of Written Text

This language activity was selected because of its potential as a linguistically contextualized language discourse event. The focus during this discourse situation was on the audience's role in imposing language demands on the student presenters. Again, teacher and peer questioning styles and response patterns were noted to gauge the degree of audience distance or proximity. This classroom event occurred in approximately 40 percent of all social studies lessons observed and in both English and Spanish.

The chief function of this language activity was to present students with a classroom language situation in which they could practice and develop their oral presentation and audience listening skills. During this discourse event, the students were expected either to talk through or read their written compositions.

The usual procedure for this language activity began with a composition task, with the topic selected by the teacher. Normally, the teacher provided sentence starters or other suggestions about topics and points to be included in the composition task (for instance, "Today we're going to write on the following topic: 'In the year 2010, I plan to . . . '"). The students were allowed to engage in the writing as a solitary activity or as a social activity in the company of a peer. Despite the conditions under which the students wrote, the teacher recommended that they read or talk through their compositions with a partner before formally presenting their work to the class.

Formal presentations required reorganizing the classroom seating arrangement to simulate an auditorium setting. The students usually moved their chairs to the middle of the classroom in rows. In general, because few students volunteered, the teacher was forced to select, as well as to convince, students to stand at the front of the class and either read or talk from their written texts. After individual students presented, they were usually asked to field questions from the "audience"—their peers and teacher.

My analysis of language use focused on the role the audience (teacher and peers) played in creating the social context in which students were encouraged or required to present information in clear and explicit ways. I examined teacher and peer (audience) responses to student oral presentations using the IRE interaction sequence to categorize and quantify target student, teacher, and peer language patterns.

As discussed earlier, the teacher initiated this discourse event, and the students selected were expected to present their narratives orally. The students' narratives constituted the response (R) in the IRE sequence. Depending on the students' verbosity and enthusiasm for presenting before their peers, the teacher either probed them for additional information or opened the floor to questions.

The focus of the following discussion is on the response patterns of the teacher and peers. In other words, the focus of the analysis during this discourse event centered on the third component of the IRE interaction sequence—the evaluation. This component consisted of teacher and peer comments, questions, and conventional evaluations.

The analysis of the teacher and peer responses shows that the teacher and students reacted with different response patterns to student presentations. Nevertheless, both sets of response strategies relied on an assumed shared background with the presenter, and as a result, they failed to create a sociolinguistic situation in which demands for linguistically contextualized language were made.

Teacher Response Patterns. Teacher responses to student oral presentations of written text consisted primarily of requests for clarification, requests for information about topics not explicitly covered in the presentation, evaluations, and probing and assistance offers. Clarification requests required the students to clarify and/or elaborate upon their presentations. Requests for information about topics not covered in the presentation referred to requests for information based on the teacher's additional knowledge about the information presented. Teacher probing and offers of assistance refer to the teacher's efforts at either elaborating on or extending the students' discourse. The teacher evaluations, similar to those on the oral vocabulary and definition activities, tended to be positive and accepting.

For example, 36 percent of the teacher's responses consisted of requests for clarification. The teacher's preferred questions—clarification questions—created opportunities for the presenters to clarify previously unclear or ambiguous discourse. Hypothetically, this type of question encourages speakers and writers to take an audience perspective and, as a result, to distance themselves from their discourse text in order to render it more explicit.

Unfortunately, this type of questioning strategy occurred only 36 percent of the time and did not serve consistently to elicit linguistically contextualized language from the students. Perhaps if the teacher had relied on this strategy more often and had not offset its effects by relying on many other less-demanding evaluations, the students would have used more explicit and linguistically contextualized language. This failure occurred primarily because the teacher's other preferred responses and questions adversely affected or neutralized the creation of a consistent, linguistically demanding social context, as illustrated in the following questions (translations are italicized):

After student explained that her group at camp had gotten first place . . .
TEACHER: ¿Para qué eran los puntos? (*What were the points for?*)

After student shared that he had eaten in a cafeteria that served a
variety of food . . .
TEACHER: ¿Fué como en la cafeteria que todo dan? (*Was it like in
that cafeteria where all types of food are served?*)

I also observed that for this activity, the teacher's second preferred
question strategy was to request unknown information. Twenty percent
of the teacher responses were requests for information not covered in
the student presentation. Usually, this type of question serves to advance the student narrative because speakers are required to supply additional information. However, since these particular questions requested information not explicitly mentioned by the speaker, it is likely
that the listener was relying on knowledge beyond that formally presented in order to pose the question.

Further, this type of question was based on the listener's real or assumed shared knowledge. For example, one student's presentation focused on his fifth-grade camping experiences. Specifically, the student
discussed the many sports activities he participated in (fishing, rafting,
and so on). Following his presentation, the teacher requested information regarding the student's bunking situation: "How did all you guys in
your cabin get along?" This kind of question can be perceived as either
slightly irrelevant or as relying on implicitly shared information (such as
knowledge of the camp's living arrangements).

One result of this questioning strategy can be to encourage assumptions about shared background information between the presenter and
the audience. Therefore, instead of encouraging overt explicitness and
clarity, questions of this type may very well yield the opposite, in the
form of less-explicit responses. The teacher's questioning style did not
help create a discourse situation in which the students felt the need to
stretch to distance themselves from the audience and to distinguish between the message being transmitted versus the interaction with the audience. In addition, the question format employed by the teacher often
precluded any real possibility for discourse elaboration in that the
teacher-preferred responses consisted of conventional evaluations: Fif-
teen percent of these responses were composed of evaluations. The
evaluations were usually positive in nature and communicated the
teacher's acceptance of the students' presentations and the appropriateness of their narratives:

After two students presented their essays on "one day we had to
leave . . ." and after audience applause . . .
TEACHER: Congratulations, Luis.
TEACHER: Good job, Jason.

During the teacher-student interaction, I also observed that 14 percent of the teacher's responses consisted of offers of assistance. The teacher frequently reiterated or clarified sections of the student presentations. She did require the students to clarify their own discourse, although she more often modeled clarification strategies for the students herself. Unfortunately, although she may have had expectations that the students would generate linguistically contextualized language, she did not give them explicit instructions on how to do so. The teacher neither informed the students explicitly of the intentions of her efforts nor did she require that they emulate her language behavior.

The role of the teacher as audience during student oral presentations of written text was characterized as quite collaborative in nature. The majority of the teacher responses to the student presenters assumed and promoted the assumption of shared knowledge between presenter and audience, which proved to be false. The teacher seldom communicated to the students explicitly that their narratives were vague or unclear, thus leading to a form of misteaching. In fact, her evaluations were usually positive, even though the answers provided by the students were not always clear or correct. Although the teacher at times modeled appropriate linguistically contextualized language strategies to render narratives more explicit and coherent, she did not communicate her intention clearly, and she did not immediately require the students to emulate her linguistic modeling.

My analysis of the teacher's response patterns suggests that, most likely, the students perceived their language performance to be appropriate and did not understand the importance of producing clear and overtly explicit oral texts. In addition, in spite of the teacher's efforts to create a "formal" academic setting in which students could refine their presentation skills, the students did not have the opportunity to practice presenting to a viable imaginary distant audience. Peer responses to student oral presentations of written text were similarly collaborative and dependent on shared knowledge between the presenter and the audience.

Peer Preferred Responses. The most frequent peer questions consisted of requests for unknown information and humorous questions or responses; 41 percent of all student questions consisted of requests for unknown information. Like teacher requests, student requests for unknown information have the potential to advance students' narratives because the presenters are asked for elaboration. However, since the request was usually for a topic or subject not presented by the speaker, it is likely that the audience was relying on knowledge other than that presented. Requests for unknown information are often based on the listener's assumptions of knowledge shared with the speaker:[8]

Student presentation:
One bright June morning in the year 2010, I will be 23 years old. I
 will have a nice red convertible and my own apartment. My life
 will be happy except that I will have to get up early every day to
 go to work. (Felice)
Peer responses to student presentation:
STUDENT 1: Will you be married?
STUDENT 2: Will you have children?

Another type of peer response during student oral presentations of
written text consisted of humorous or facetious requests for additional
information. Approximately 30 percent of the peer responses were of
this type. In the resultant informal discourse situation, in which the
dominant tone was one of fun and jocularity, the focus continued to be
on the interaction between presenter and audience instead of on the information being transmitted, as exemplified in this student's oral presentation of a hypothetical situation:

Student presentation:
We had to move because too many people were coming and were
 living where we were living and the path that we were going to
 take was blocked. So we took the other path. . . . When we decided to leave we took our chairs, our cattle, our land, our house
 and our family, our table and when we were going we had trouble
 because my Mom would get sick. There was no doctor. We had to
 cross the Mississippi River . . . we hoped to find a house, animals,
 land, food . . . and a place for the children to play. (Evaristo)
STUDENT 1: Did anyone hijack your horse? (elicits laughter)
STUDENT 2: Why is it so quiet? (elicits laughter)

Peers also responded to student oral presentations of written text by
asking questions about known information and by requesting clarification. For example, 19 percent of the peer responses were requests for
known information, and 11 percent were requests for clarification.
 The role of peers as audience was similar to that of the teacher during
student oral presentations of written text. The audience's role was also
characterized as quite collaborative. The majority of peer responses
consisted of requests for unknown information. Audience responses of
this type established an informal, almost jocular atmosphere in which
there was little need for students to concern themselves with producing
overtly explicit and clear narratives.
 Very few of the peer responses required the students to clarify or extend their discourse to render their language more comprehensible and

clear. Instead, the audience participation promoted the discourse event as an informal social situation during which the students could socialize and joke with one another. As a result, the students produced little or no linguistically contextualized language.

The audience in this discourse situation had the potential to help create an academic context by confronting students with questions that would require their conscious consideration of audience needs regarding coherent and clear text. Hypothetically, the students might be expected to react by modifying their language when faced with such linguistic requirements. However, analysis of audience questions and responses in this study shows that the need for presenters to linguistically contextualize their language was not obvious. Rather, both teacher and peers proved themselves quite willing to assume shared background knowledge to assist the presenter. Except for the requests for clarification and the questions for known information asked by both teacher and peers, there were few instances when the audience demanded that the presenter treat it as a distant and nonresponsive interlocutor. Furthermore, it is important to note that the instances in which teacher and peers required the students to expand and clarify their language use were few compared to their more informal ways of responding. Thus, the linguistic input present in this language-teaching context was rather insufficient in terms of enabling students to acquire both the academic discourse and the necessary pragmatic strategies for its use. The only true opportunity for the students to interact with a viable distant audience was when they engaged in solitary writing activities, but in this case, no real audience was present to let them know that further information was needed.

Solitary Writing Activities

The third discourse event selected for study consisted of student solitary writing activities. This type of writing activity differed from the foregoing (oral presentation of written text) in that the students were engaged in a writing task as a solitary activity with little input from peers and teacher. In addition, there was no oral presentation component. In fact, the process was a more traditional one, in which the students wrote in isolation and relied on Cortland's written comments for feedback. Children in elementary school are frequently asked to write pieces that require some degree of writer distance from the intended audience.[9] Often, teachers (like the one in this study) request that students write to imaginary distant audiences about personal topics—topics relating to the students themselves and to people they know (friends, relatives, teacher, and so forth). This type of personal writing is closer to everyday speech than impersonal writing (for example, expository writing activities such as describing science experiments), and it is the kind of writing that children produce first, to the extent that complete impersonal writing is not usually found until the third year of secondary school.

Precisely this type of elementary personal writing was observed in the classroom. The students wrote on a variety of topics, including pioneer life in the old West, letters to a real or imaginary grandmother, and mini-autobiographies.

Once the students completed their essays, they submitted their work to Cortland, who later corrected it. At times, the teacher required the students to rewrite their essays, incorporating her corrections and suggestions. At other times, she simply corrected the work and returned it to the students.

The teacher's evaluations of the essays focused on surface features, such as spelling errors and punctuation. Seldom did Cortland's corrections or comments focus on the clarity or coherence of the written text. Forty-one percent of her evaluations focused on correctness of spelling; 36 percent focused on correct punctuation; and 19 percent mentioned other aspects of grammar (for example, Spanish accent marks). Only four percent of Cortland's comments concerned editing or the restructuring of text.

Solitary writing discourse events occurred in both English and Spanish and were observed in approximately 66 percent of all the language arts lessons I observed. I focused on writing assignments that were open-ended essays, in which students wrote extensively and were expected to communicate a message to a distant audience. (I did not examine more restrictive writing assignments, such as worksheet and workbook writing activities, although these types of assignments occurred even more frequently across subject areas than the solitary writing assignments.)

The boundaries of solitary writing activities were marked by Cortland in two ways. Because the teacher had incorporated a journal-writing period into the regular classroom schedule, students knew they were expected to write in their journals every day for approximately 20 minutes. When the students returned to the classroom after recess, Cortland usually had a sentence started on the blackboard, signaling the topic on which they were expected to write. The following are examples of journal sentence starters: *Un día me fuí de viaje* . . . (One day I left on a trip . . .); *Un día me encontré en el laboratorio de un científico inventor y le preguntó* . . . (One day I met an inventor/scientist in a laboratory and I asked him/her . . .)

During the journal-writing activity, Cortland initiated a regular writing routine, which the students quickly adopted. After the 20-minute period was over, either Cortland verbally signaled the close of the writing session or the students themselves noted the time and responded by putting their journals away and preparing for the next academic subject, without prompting from the teacher. When the writing period was shortened or when the students did not initiate the closing, the teacher marked the closing of the period. The following is an example of a teacher-initiated closing: *"OK clase, ya es hora de entregar nuestro trabajo escrito. Favor de pasarlo hacía adelante"* (OK class, it's time to hand in our written work. Please pass your work forward).

During nonjournal writing assignments, Cortland again verbally marked the opening and closing of the discourse events. In lieu of a sentence starter, she often provided the students with an elaborate scenario meant to provide them with a context for their next writing assignment. The following is an example of the teacher's extensive opening statement (translation is italicized):

Ahora, ya llegaron a su nueva casa. Ya han estado trabajando duro, duro para construír, buscar madera porque allá no había, para hacer adobes, ladrillos y lo necesario para sembrar maíz, papas, trigo y todo para cuidar bien a los caballos . . . la abejas para hacer miel . . . y ahora parece que va a haber correo. ¿Qué es correo? (Students respond "Mail?") Sí, y parece que hay un señor en un caballo . . . y va a recoger correo.

Y estás pensando en tu abuela—que le pasa allá, allá atrás. Y hace un año que no has visto a tu abuela.

Vamos a imaginar que le vamos a escribir una carta, a dar vuelo contandole todo lo que ha pasado este año. Como, por ejemplo, como te sentistes al tener que dejar tu casa. Todo lo que vistes en el viaje, todo lo bonito de viaje. ¿Tienes nuevos amigos? ¿Has aprendido cosas nuevas? Los trabajos que tienen que hacer ahora.

Quiero que cuando hagan esta parte que se acuerden que allí arriba va la dirección del rémite . . . y después la fecha, y luego va el saludo. Y en esta parte va . . . Mariana, ¿cómo le vamos a poner al saludo? (Student does not respond.) "A mi abuelita." ¿Hay preguntas? Pueden escribir su dirección de ahora o pueden inventar una nueva dirección que podrían tener allá en el oeste . . . ¿Hay preguntas? Pues, empiezen.

(Now, you've arrived at your new home. You have been working hard, hard, in order to build, to find lumber because there was none there, in order to make adobe, bricks and everything else that was necessary to grow corn, potatoes, wheat and everything necessary to care for the horses . . . the bees to make honey . . . and now it seems there is going to be mail. What is mail? (Students respond "Mail?") Yes, and it looks like there is a man on a horse who is going to collect mail.

And you're thinking about your grandmother—how she is doing back there. And it's been a year that you haven't seen your grandmother.

Let's imagine that we're going to write her a letter telling her everything that has happened this year. Like for example, how you felt when you had to leave your home, everything you saw on your trip, all the beautiful experiences of the trip. Do you have new friends? Have you learned new things? The types of new jobs you have to do now.

When you begin your letter, I want you to remember that the return address goes up here . . . then the date, and then the salutation. And on this part you write . . . Mariana, what are we going to write as the salutation? (No student response.) "To my grandmother." Are there any questions? You can write your real address or you can invent a new address that you could possibly have had in the old West. Are there any questions? Well then, begin (social studies).

As can be discerned, Cortland opened the writing session with elaborate instructions and assistance. She provided the writing assignment topic as well as numerous examples for the students to include in their narratives. In addition, she usually marked the close of nonjournal writing activities. The following is an example of a closing marker: "I'd like to say 'congratulations' for the very nice work and behavior. I'd also like to call your attention to the fact that Friday is a field trip for all of you that are on community service".

The solitary writing activities occurred across a variety of academic subjects. The chief purpose of solitary writing activities was to increase the students' enjoyment of writing and to provide them with opportunities to improve their writing ability. The language mode focused upon in this discourse event was written language.

The students' writing was examined using both a grammatical and a narrative analysis. A grammatical analysis yields information about the linguistic complexity of the text produced. The results were quite interesting and include the following:

Characteristics of Student Written Text. A grammatical analysis yielded information about the linguistic complexity and descriptive quality of student written narratives. The texts analyzed consisted only of those writing samples produced by the eight target students. During formal composition activities, students were often allowed to write in the language of their preference. For example, even if the instruction language of the day was Spanish, the students had the option of writing their compositions in either English or Spanish. However, it must be noted that on "English days," most of the students opted to write in English.

The grammatical analysis was conducted on one classroom writing assignment. This particular assignment required the students to write an imaginary letter to their grandmother describing the trials and tribulations they experienced as pioneer children.

The students' written pieces varied in length but in general were not long or complex. The t-units were short (as measured by mean length of utterance [MLU]) and were linguistically simple. The students performed similarly across achievement groups. The students averaged 106.71 words, 16.00 t-units per text, and an average MLU of 6.43. Student language was not particularly descriptive. In addition, the students averaged less than one adjective per t-unit (.71). The students' written texts were linguistically simple and were not particularly descriptive or coherent, as shown in the following examples (all student letters have been corrected for spelling to facilitate reading):

Dear Grandma,
I miss you a lot. I wish you could come visit me but I know you can't. Maybe I can go over if my mom lets me and if I can go I will be there in two weeks. We will have a lot of fun together going to the park and shopping. Let's see, I am going to go to sixth grade next year at Balboa [school]. I am 10 going on 11 next year too. In class we wrote a story in class and it goes like this. We had to move because there was too many people in our town. We had to leave our furniture, animals and house. We traveled. Mom got sick and Dad too so I drove the wagon. When we got there we wanted to find furniture, gold, wood to make the house, food, water and land. The horses got sick when we got there and we had to shoot them. When the house was done we lived happily ever after.

> Sincerely yours,
> Blanca

P.S. Mom and Dad got well and write back.

Dear Grandmother,
I hope I could see you again. I hope you are OK when you live alone. I wish I could see my old house again. It was hard and boring to go to school. I live in a big house. It's been at least a year I never see you. It took almost a year to get home. Then the Indians wanted to attack. We won, we had guns. Then we got hijacked and got a rifle and bullets. When the Indians came again to attack they didn't have bullets but the Indians lived. It took a long time to get some [illegible], we got stuck in a river. The wagon got stuck. It took at least 10 minutes to get free then the wheel fell down. They fixed it. I had lots of fun when I got home and went swimming.

> Sincerely,
> Joey

In spite of the potential for this academic discourse event to create in the students the need to communicate with a viable audience (for example, a real or imaginary grandmother), students did not linguistically contextualize their language in conventional ways. Instead, they wrote halfheartedly and confused present occurrences with imaginary past incidents. The students treated the assignment as a simulated writing activity rather than an authentic writing activity. Carole Edelsky has distinguished between simulated and authentic writing activities. As she explained, in authentic writing, "the language is being used to make meaning for some purpose," but simulated writing activities do not clearly have a communicative purpose.[10] The only purpose of a simulated writing activity is the completion of the assignment or the product.

The contrast between authentic and simulated writing in school may arise from the differentiated teacher-student power relations and the inability of students to initiate and take control of their writing.[11] This disempowerment of students results in their disengaging from the writing assignment. In this case, the students wrote letters that lacked cohesiveness and coherence. Often, they incorporated Cortland's suggested inclusions and then wrote about current personal matters but made little effort to either connect or disconnect the two trains of thought.

In spite of the problems students had with the texts at the global level, Cortland's comments reflected her concerns with local-level issues (for example, correct spelling and punctuation). Thus, she reinforced in the children the importance of a "correct" product rather than the importance of drafting a text that took into consideration audience, topic development, and logic.[12] As far as the students could discern, their texts were appropriate except for the local-level errors indicated by the teacher.

As with the two other discourse events studied, the teacher did not communicate to the students the importance of planning their discourse consciously to render it as explicit as possible. Instead, the students wrote with apparent disregard of the reader's or audience's needs. They seldom edited their work, and the teacher's focus on spelling and punctuation apparently did not alert the students to reader or audience needs.

Despite the potential for the three discourse events to elicit student production of linguistically contextualized language, the classroom situation itself did not require the students to do so. In fact, little explicit emphasis was attached to lessons in which students could verbally or in writing exhibit their knowledge more effectively. Classroom language use was restricted, as previous literature on classroom discourse has described.[13] The need for students to linguistically contextualize their oral and written language simply did not exist.

Across discourse events, Cortland proved to be an extremely collaborative interlocutor and audience and accepted students' brief and incomplete responses as appropriate. The problem with this approach is that by not making the object of knowledge explicit, she not only undermined her collaborative and supporting style but also possibly stifled students' epistemological curiosity. During vocabulary and definition activities, she appeared interested in learning whether the students understood the meaning of words, not whether they conveyed the "proper" academic verbalization of that knowledge.

During student oral presentations of written text, Cortland's limited efforts at eliciting student clarification and elaboration were offset by the jocular and informal context of the event. Teacher and peers asked questions that were slightly irrelevant and, at times, humorous and facetious. The final result was that the students were not required to linguistically contextualize their texts for the benefit of audience understanding.

During solitary writing tasks, the students wrote linguistically simple texts that were neither cohesive nor coherent. They made little effort to edit and modify their texts to communicate better with the distant reader or audience. In addition, the teacher's comments made little reference to global aspects of the text; instead, they focused on local issues, such as correct spelling and punctuation. Thus, because of the linguistically restrictive nature of classroom discourse events, the students were not encouraged to demonstrate their ability to produce linguistically contextualized language, as they later did on the language tasks (see Chapter 5 for a more in-depth discussion of student performance on linguistically contextualized language tasks).

The sad irony is that schools, even under the best of circumstances, generally fail to teach linguistic-minority students in ways that will enable them to develop not only English language proficiency but also the more pertinent class-based academic discourse. By not understanding the interplay between class and language, teachers often end up reproducing those middle-class-specific language behaviors that often fail to promote psychologically harmless language learning contexts. In fact, in many instances, teachers' false assumptions concerning students classroom discourse competency could also produce a form of resistance, as demonstrated in the example provided by Dell Hymes or in my own case study. In other words, not only do teachers, even when they are well intentioned, often fail to successfully teach the academic discourse necessary for school success, they also show no understanding of how to use students' potential language resistance as a pedagogical tool that could maximize learning. This is partly but not totally due to the false assumptions in the preparation of language teachers that present language as a neutral entity and as merely a vehicle of communication that is equally available to all. Thus, language teaching often emphasizes the technical dimensions of language while disembedding it from the sociocultural and class contexts that generate and shape each discourse reality. As a consequence, the entrapment pedagogy runs much deeper than requiring of students what the teacher does not teach them. The teachers are also victims of this entrapment in that they have been inculcated with myths about the nature of language that not only de-skill the teachers themselves but also prevent them from understanding the asymmetrical power relations hidden in the ideological web of multiple discourse manipulation.

5 Student Language Performance on Language Tasks

In the preceding chapters, particularly Chapter 1, I problematized the notions of "*de*-contextualized" language versus "contextualized" language. In this chapter, however, I use these categories as part of the current paradigm of research studying the so-called *de*-contextualized or contextualized language. What follows is a description of the linguistic performance of eight target students on two language tasks designed specifically to elicit linguistically contextualized language. The target students include four students each from the higher- and lower-achieving ability groups (designated as such by their performance on standardized tests). The children identified as higher-achieving students were: Marissa Nava, Miguel Lara, Blanca Mariscal, and Evaristo Parra. The children identified as lower-achieving students were: Felice Villalpando, Oscar Loaíza, Raquel Ibarra, and Joey Elenes. (A more detailed profile of these students is given in Chapter 3.) The children were administered a battery of language tasks specifically designed to tap their ability to linguistically contextualize their language.

Given the classroom findings discussed in the previous chapter, it appears that, although the teacher did her best to create discourse events likely to elicit linguistically contextualized language, the children transformed the discourse events into informal ones that did not require their production of overtly precise and explicit language. In addition, despite the teacher's frustration that the children did not produce this type of language, she failed to explicitly discuss with them the importance of developing overtly explicit and precise discourse skills. It was difficult to discern, given the teacher-student reconfiguration of the discourse events, whether and how the children go about linguistically contextualizing their language in contexts that require them to communicate with distant audiences.

To learn whether the children could, indeed, produce linguistically contextualized language so as to provide overtly precise and explicit utterances, it was necessary to create language contexts that more authentically demanded that they address believable distant audiences. Given time constraints, I decided to administer a battery of language tasks to the eight target students. These consisted of two general language tasks and subtasks. The two general language tasks included picture description and definition tasks. Specifically, I administered four picture description subtasks and one noun definition task, all versions of the tasks developed by Catherine Snow and her associates.[1] I administered all tasks in both English and Spanish, during separate sessions.

This component of my research produced four major findings related to linguistically contextualized language production. The findings address my interest in learning whether the target students could, indeed, linguistically contextualize their language and, if so, how they went about doing this. In addition, I also examined whether there were differences between the two groups in terms of the ability to linguistically contextualize language.

The four general findings suggest that, across ability groups: (1) the students made efforts to linguistically contextualize their language when communicating with distant versus present audiences; (2) the students were better able to linguistically contextualize their language orally rather than in written form; (3) the students were able to linguistically contextualize in both English and Spanish, although the higher achievers produced more linguistically contextualized language in English and the lower achievers did so in Spanish; and (4) the students proved to be adequate communicators when language form (such as the ability to linguistically contextualize) was not taken into consideration.

Across achievement groups, the students recognized and modified their language when describing pictures to imaginary distant versus present audience. They modified their language similarly in English and Spanish. In general, the higher-achieving students consistently produced slightly *more* linguistically contextualized language (as measured by t-unit and narrative strategy production) on the English picture description tasks, and the lower-achieving group produced slightly more such language on the Spanish picture description tasks. This occurred in spite of the fact that both groups of students were classified as equally proficient in English and Spanish and differed only in their standardized test performances. Achievement-group language preference held true on the picture description and definition tasks. For a better understanding of these general findings, it is necessary to return to the specific language tasks and examine student language use patterns for each of the tasks.

Picture Description Tasks

The purpose of the picture description tasks was to examine the students' descriptions under two types of sociolinguistic conditions: "one in which language is lodged in a conversational context that supports effective communication, and one in which, because context is not overt, successful communication is contingent upon language alone, rather than upon any physical context or opportunity for clarification."[2] For this task, students were asked to describe pictures under four different conditions that clearly distinguished between providing information to a physically present audience and providing information to an imaginary distant audience. In other words, I presented students with oral and written language tasks (in both English and Spanish) that required them to describe pictures to both present and imaginary distant audiences. This task included presenting subjects with four color illustrations (two for eliciting responses in English and two in Spanish), one at a time. The pictures were originally taken from children's storybooks, and all contained two or more characters in the process of performing various actions. Students were asked to describe the various pictures under four social conditions:

1. Oral contextualized (picture described orally to a present audience): The child was asked to describe a picture to the researcher, who was seated near the child, could see the picture, and gave appropriate conversational responses, including clarification questions and collaborative discussion of the picture.

2. Written contextualized (picture described in writing to a present audience): The child was asked to write a description of a picture underneath the picture itself, so that a potential reader could see the referent while reading the child's description.

3. Oral linguistically contextualized (picture described orally to a distant audience): The child was asked to record the description of a picture on a tape recorder, so that it could later be played to someone who had never seen the picture and who would draw a representation of that same picture on the basis of the child's description.

4. Written linguistically contextualized (picture described in writing to a distant audience): The child was asked to write a description of a picture for someone unfamiliar with the picture, who would be expected to draw a representation of the same picture based on the child's written description. Under this condition, the child wrote the description on a sheet of paper physically separate from the picture.[3]

I expected the students' language to be more overtly precise and explicit when I asked them to describe the pictures to imaginary distant audiences and less so when describing the pictures to me, an audience present and familiar with the pictures. In general, my hunches proved correct; I found that when the students were required to share information about the pictures with distant audiences, they produced more language in general (more t-units); more descriptive words, such as adjectives and adverbs (descriptors); and a greater number of narrative strategies (such as the use of locative phrases) to produce what they considered appropriately linguistically contextualized responses. I discuss the students' use of these three linguistic contextualizing strategies on the picture description tasks in the next sections, followed by a discussion of the students' language performance on the noun definition task.

Students' Use of Linguistic Contextualizing Strategies

Across the language tasks, all of the target students were able to modify their language use when addressing distant audiences. In sociolinguistic contexts, where it was clear that they were expected to share information with a listener not physically present, they incorporated a greater number of linguistically contextualized language strategies to render their messages overtly explicit. Although they generally tended to assume shared knowledge with their interlocutors and to rely on contextualized language to convey their messages, most of the students did produce linguistically contextualized language at times. They demonstrated this ability on language tasks that required them to communicate with a believable distant audience. When this requirement was mandatory, the students made a greater linguistic effort to produce messages in an overtly clear and explicit manner. However, the higher achievers proved to be slightly more sophisticated in their use of linguistically contextualized language than their lower-achieving peers. The following sections describe the two group's (1) general language production, (2) use of describing words, and (3) employment of narrative strategies in both English and Spanish on the four picture description tasks. After describing the two group's language performance in general terms, I provide actual samples of students' descriptions in order to illustrate the general findings discussed here.

General Language (T-Unit) Production. Across the four English picture description tasks, both achievement groups produced a greater amount of language in general (as measured by mean average of t-units) on the English oral picture description to a distant audience task than on the other three. That is, all of the children produced more language on tasks that explicitly required that they accurately describe a picture to an imaginary audience with no access to the picture. Although all of the children performed similarly in terms of greater language produc-

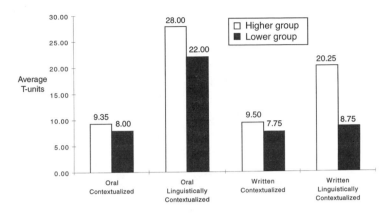

Picture Description Tasks

FIGURE 5.1   *Student T-Unit Production on English Picture Description Tasks*

tion, some ability-group differences surfaced. It is evident that the higher-achieving students produced more total language on the English tasks than did the lower achievement group.

For example, the higher achievement group produced a mean average of 28 t-units on the English oral linguistically contextualized task, compared to 20.25 on the English written linguistically contextualized task, 9.35 on the English oral contextualized task, and 9.50 on the English written contextualized task (see Figure 5.1). Clearly, these students produced more language on the oral linguistically contextualized task, the written linguistically contextualized task, the oral contextualized task, and finally, the written contextualized task.

The lower-achieving group produced a mean average of 22 t-units on the English oral linguistically contextualized task, compared to 8.75 on the English written linguistically contextualized task, 8.0 on the English oral contextualized task, and 7.75 on the English written contextualized task.

Although the sample size was too small to attempt to test for statistical significance in mean difference, the numbers suggest that the students were similar in their ability to linguistically contextualize in the English oral mode (higher achievement group's 28 t-units versus lower achievement group's 22 t-units). However, ability-group differences in English writing ability appear to be significant when we compare t-units produced on the linguistically contextualized *written* task (higher achievement group's 20.25 t-units and lower achievements group's 8.75). Despite their production of less language, the lower-achieving students basically followed the same pattern of language production as did their higher-achieving peers: They produced the most language on the En-

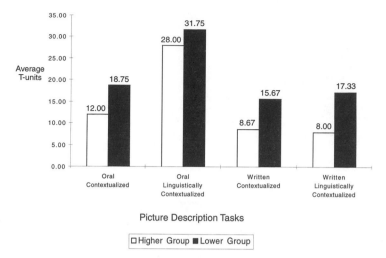

FIGURE 5.2 *Student Production on Spanish Picture Description Tasks*

glish oral linguistically contextualized task, followed by the written linguistically contextualized task, then the oral contextualized task, and finally, the written contextualized task.

Similar language patterns were observed on the Spanish picture description tasks. The students continued to use more language (t-units) on tasks that explicitly required them to describe pictures to viable distant audiences than on those that did not. It is interesting, however, that on the Spanish tasks, the students from the lower-achieving group produced more language than their higher-achieving peers.

As with the English picture description tasks, the results here indicate that all of the students continued to produce a greater number of t-units on the Spanish oral linguistically contextualized tasks. The higher-achieving group produced a mean average of 28.00 t-units on the oral linguistically contextualized task, 12.00 on the Spanish oral contextualized task, 8.67 on the Spanish written contextualized task, and 8.00 on the Spanish written linguistically contextualized task (see Figure 5.2).

This group's performance in language production patterns differed slightly from their performance on the English language tasks. That is, similar to their performance on the English task, they produced most of their language on the oral linguistically contextualized task. However, the next highest level of language production was elicited by the oral contextualized language task, not the linguistically contextualized written task. This finding suggests that it is possible that the higher-achieving students were orally proficient in Spanish but did not necessarily possess the Spanish writing skills necessary to render their writing overtly explicit and precise, as they had done in English.

The lower-achieving group also followed the higher-ability group's language production pattern. This group produced a mean average of 31.75 t-units on the Spanish oral linguistically contextualized task, 18.75 on the Spanish oral contextualized task, 15.67 on the Spanish written contextualized task, and 17.33 on the Spanish written linguistically contextualized task. Again, the sample size was too small to test for significance in mean differences. Nevertheless, the lower-achieving group produced more language than their higher-achieving peers (31.75 versus 28.00 on the Spanish linguistically contextualized oral task; 18.75 versus 12.00 on the Spanish oral contextualized task; 15.67 versus 8.67 on the Spanish written contextualized task; and 17.33 versus 8.0 on the Spanish linguistically contextualized written task).

Despite the difference in language production by ability group, the two group's resembled each other in pattern of language production: They produced more language on both the oral tasks than on the tasks that required them to write, although the lower-achieving students produced much more language on the oral linguistically contextualized task than on the oral contextualized task. These findings strongly suggest that the lower-achieving students may be more proficient in Spanish that the higher-achievement group. However, similar to their higher-achieving peers, the lower-achieving students also produced more language on both oral tasks than on the written ones, suggesting that their Spanish verbal ability may be stronger than their writing skills in Spanish.

Narrative Strategies. As part of my analyses, I also examined the students' use of three narrative strategies commonly employed to render narratives overtly explicit and precise. I focused on students' use of an introductory sentence that specified the context or setting of the picture being described, as well as the production of both locatives and clarificatory markers.[4] Across languages and tasks, the students seldom employed an introductory sentence specifying the pictures' contexts or settings in their descriptions, as exemplified by Marissa's writing, "This picture is about five kids," and Oscar's writing, "One day the mother pig was making breakfast for her sons and daughters." More often than not, the students employed less-explicit ways of opening their picture descriptions, such as Oscar's "Hay tres niños cortando un palo" (There are three boys cutting a tree) and Felice's "I think the kids are playing with different kinds of rocks and shells." The students provided some locatives and, less frequently, clarificatory markers.

Across achievement groups, the students seldom employed either type of introduction strategy. This tendency is significant because the literature suggests that middle-class white students of this age frequently specify setting and utilize locatives and clarificatory strategies to render their discourse more coherent and explicit.[5] Nevertheless, despite the students' limited use of these two types of introductory strategies, they tended to utilize locatives on the linguistically contextualized tasks rather than on the contextualized tasks.

The higher achievers utilized more locatives on tasks that required that they communicate with distant audiences. This group produced a mean average of 4.50 locatives on the oral linguistically contextualized task, 4.25 locatives on the written linguistically contextualized task, 3.75 locatives on the written contextualized tasks, and 1.25 locatives on the oral contextualized task.

The greater use of locatives on the written contextualized tasks suggests that the students must realize that, despite the fact that they were communicating with a *present* audience using the written mode, *written* communication generally requires more explicit language than is usually required in a similar situation requiring the oral mode. Thus, at least for the higher-achieving group, mode appeared to supersede the type of audience being communicated with. The following examples of locative use are taken from the target students' descriptions:

> They're in a bowling alley.
> They're on the floor.
> There is long grass next to the sand. (Marissa Nava)
> One of them is on the left hand [side] and the other one is on the right hand side.
> They are on the beach and on the sand.
> The knife is on the table next to the bread. (Joey Ibarra)

The lower achievers did not consistently utilize locatives as a way of linguistically contextualizing their picture descriptions. As shown in the previous analyses, the lower-achieving group produced fewer locatives across the English picture description tasks than did the higher achievers. However, this group, similar to the higher achievers, also relied more on the production of locatives than other narrative strategies (such as describing the setting and using clarificatory markers) to render their language overtly explicit. The lower-achieving students produced, on average, 4.75 locatives on the English oral linguistically contextualized task, 3.50 on the English written contextualized task, and 3.25 on the English written linguistically contextualized task.

My analysis of student production of narrative strategies on the Spanish picture description tasks showed, once again, that the students produced more of these strategies on the linguistically contextualized tasks. In the higher-achieving group's production of narrative strategies on the

Spanish picture description tasks, introductory sentences and clarificatory markers were almost nonexistent. Of the three strategies, locatives
were most frequently employed by the higher achievers. In fact, the majority of locatives (a mean average of 6.33) were produced on the oral
linguistically contextualized task.

The lower-achieving students also produced few or no introductory
sentences that included explicit information about the picture's context
or setting. They employed clarificatory markers more frequently on the
oral linguistically contextualized task (a mean average of 3.00) and produced locatives more often on both linguistically contextualized tasks. A
mean average of 7.50 locatives resulted on the oral linguistically contextualized task and 6.00 on the written linguistically contextualized tasks.

The picture description results clearly show that the students produced more language and narrative strategies (specifically, locatives) on
the picture description tasks requiring them to communicate with distant audiences. When the students were asked to describe pictures to
distant audiences, they attempted, across achievement groups, to modify their language to produce overtly explicit and comprehensible descriptions. The students demonstrated a greater ability to linguistically
contextualize their language orally than in written fashion. When the
language tasks did not require them to communicate with distant audiences, they relied more on contextualized communication.

Clearly, the students from both achievement groups demonstrated
the ability (both verbally and in writing) to distinguish tasks that required them to communicate with distant versus present audiences, although their ability to do so in the oral mode was greater than their ability to do so in the written mode. In general, the students produced more
language and locatives to render their picture descriptions overtly explicit and precise when describing them to a distant instead of a present
audience. In the next section, I share examples of three students' picture
descriptions, followed by a more in-depth discussion, to illustrate the
general trends described thus far.

Three Student Picture Descriptions:
Evaristo, Marissa, and Oscar

The chief purpose for including three samples of students' actual picture descriptions across ability groups and in both languages is to make
more concrete my rather abstract discussion of the findings in the preceding section. The picture description samples exemplify the target
students' tendency to utilize more linguistically contextualized strategies on descriptions meant for distant audiences rather than present
ones. In addition, their stronger ability to linguistically contextualize in

the oral mode rather than in the written mode becomes evident as the reader reviews each set of picture descriptions in both English and Spanish. Two of the picture descriptions are in English and were produced by Evaristo Parra, a higher-achieving student, and by Oscar Loaíza, a lower-achieving student. The Spanish picture description was produced by Marissa Nava, a high-achieving student. Marissa was selected because her descriptions were typical of both higher- and lower-achieving students.

Evaristo Parra—High-Achieving Student.

> Oral picture description to a present audience: These two boys are trying to grab lambs and trying to take 'em. Then it looks like this dog came and jumped on this boy. And there's this other dog waiting for this boy and he's scared so he's backing off. And then there's the water . . . people running. This guy gots a big [unintelligible] and a bottle to throw at the dog. This other guy, this guy right here [taps the illustration] is getting attacked by 'em. And he's rolling over yelling for help so he comes and tries to save him but this other dog comes. He comes and waits for him so if he makes any sudden moves, he'll come after him. That's it.

Evaristo produced a rather brief description. Although he did not explicitly describe the physical setting in which the action took place, in the first sentence he did explain that the main characters consisted of two boys and that the central activity consisted of two boys "trying to grab lambs." Evaristo was ambiguous in his use of pronouns when he explained that "there's this other dog waiting for this boy and *he's* scared so *he's* backing off." It is unclear in this sentence whether "he" referred to the *other* boy or *this* boy. The next sentence is equally unclear, for Evaristo explained "And then there's the water . . . people running" with no further elaboration, giving this part of the description an almost shopping-list quality. In addition, two sentences later, he emphatically stated, "This other guy, *this guy right here*," while tapping the picture, "is getting attacked by 'em," apparently calling the researcher's attention to an extralinguistic cue—the picture—in order to make sense of his description. Finally, he concluded his description by saying, "That's it."

Since this oral task required Evaristo to communicate with a present audience, he appeared to correctly assume that it was communicatively appropriate to rely on shared knowledge with the researcher (a present audience) about the picture while he described it. This assumption that it was appropriate to assume shared knowledge with the audience was not as apparent in his oral description to a distant audience. Evaristo's attempts to be more overtly explicit and precise by relying on greater language production, use of more semantically precise descriptors, and use of meta-level directives were evident in the next picture description.

Oral picture description to a distant audience: There's this grandpa, his grandson, and his granddaughter. They're at a bowling alley. The grandpa is getting ready to throw the ball. His arm's way up in the air with the ball already. And the granddaughter is cheering him on and the grandson is saying, "Can I try it?" But the grandfather is still laughing. He's just smiling. And they're standing right beside him. They have their bowling shoes on. The granddaughter has blue ones on and the grandpa and the grandson have red ones.

The ball, the bowling ball is blue. The pins are white and red. And there's this alley where they throw the ball—it's white and the sides, it's yellow. The grandpa has a very pointy nose. He has only, no hair on the top, just on the sides and he's very old.

He has yellow and green pants on and he has a blue jacket. The grandson has yellow hair. He has a blue jacket with yellow, one yellow stripe around the whole thing and a blue one. And that, this thing is white. This part of the jacket, it's white. And the tight things of the jacket is white. And the grandson also has a pointy nose. He has an open mouth. And now we're jumping to the granddaughter. She has brown hair. She has her hands and her arms are up. The sleeves of the jacket are white. Her pants are white too. And her jacket is red 'cept for the blue stripes—two blue stripes. And the tight thing at the end of the jacket, that tight thing is red. And there's, she has her eyes open. She has half a circle nose and she's facing this way, toward us. Her mouth is wide open, yelling like she's happy. She has short hair. And one of the pins are down. That's it!

The thing on top of the bowling thing—where the pins are, on top; there's three squares then you go, then there's a little thing separation and then there's other three squares and there's a heart colored red and the background is blue.

In this picture description, Evaristo began his narrative by introducing the three main characters in the picture: the grandpa, the grandson, and the granddaughter. The second sentences introduced the reader to the setting—the bowling alley. Evaristo also relied heavily on the use of color adjectives to render his description overtly explicit and precise. For example, in the first paragraph, he specified that the granddaughter's bowling shoes were "blue ones" and the grandson's were "red ones." In the second paragraph, he stated "the ball" and then corrected himself, "the bowling ball [which] is blue." Similarly in the rest of the text, he described the color of clothing worn by the characters and of objects present in the illustration. In addition, he demonstrated metacognitive awareness when he provided the reader with instructions in order to direct him or her. For example, in the third paragraph, he forewarned the distant reader that "now we're jumping to the granddaughter" and proceeded to describe her. He also signaled the end of the description to the reader by stating, "That's it," but then he continued to describe "the thing on top of the bowling thing" by relying chiefly on color and shape information.

In the next picture description task, Evaristo was asked to provide a written description of a picture to the researcher. Notice that he produced the least amount of total language on this task.

> Written picture description to a present audience: What I think is happening in the picture. I can see a little girl looking in her bag. This other girl is picking up rocks from the sand. The rest of the gang is collecting seashells for the collection. All of them are girls at the beach because they live near.

It appears as if the written mode of the task combined with the need to describe the picture to a present audience elicited less student language than was produced on the equivalent oral language picture description task. That is, because Evaristo described the picture to a present audience, he assumed shared knowledge (the audience also had access to the picture) and possibly concluded that an overtly explicit description was not necessary or appropriate in this communicative context. Notice that he did not provide an introductory sentence with character and setting information. In fact, he did not mention the beach setting until the last sentence. Instead, he introduced the description by explaining that he would describe what he "think[s] is happening in the picture." He then went on, in shopping-list fashion, to briefly describe what the girls were doing in the illustration.

The shortness of the written text may be due to the fact that the student can speak faster that he can write or that he may be a more proficient speaker than writer at this stage of his academic career. Despite Evaristo's tendency to produce less language on this written language task, he did produce slightly more language on the next task—the written picture description directed to a distant audience.

> Written picture description to a distant audience: There's six pigs in a kitchen. The mother pig is washing the dishes. The mother is wearing a apron. There's two pans on the counter. There's five piglet cups that have names of them. There's one blue, yellow, purple, green and red. The names are Amy, Pat, Sam, Sue and Tom's. Sue dropped a plate and broke it. Amy is giving the mother a coffee cup while Tom is drying the dishes. Pat is tasting the jam. Sam is putting away the dishes in the closet. There is a window in front of the mother. By the window there is a flower next to the curtain.

In this picture description, Evaristo appeared to understand, once again, the special communicative consideration a writer must extend to a distant reader. Unlike the previous written text in which he listed char-

acters one by one throughout the text, on this task he immediately identified the main characters and the setting in the first sentence. Similar to
his performance on the other descriptions, Evaristo relied on color descriptors and names of characters to render his description explicit and
precise. For example, he explained that the five piglet cups had the five
piglets' names on them—"Amy, Pat, Sam, Sue and Tom's"—and that they
were "blue, yellow, purple, green and red." However, unlike his performance on the oral linguistically contextualized task, Evaristo did not
employ metacognitive commentary and did not signal the end of his
picture description.

In the next section, I share Oscar Loaíza's four English picture descriptions. Despite Oscar's identification as a lower-achieving student, it is
important to notice the similarity in use of linguistic contextualizing
strategies on tasks directed to distant listeners and readers. I selected
Oscar Loaíza's English picture descriptions because they illustrate his
group's response patterns.

Oscar Loaíza—Low-Achieving Student. Across picture descriptions, it
was evident that although Oscar demonstrated general language production patterns similar to those demonstrated by Evaristo. That is, Oscar produced more language on picture descriptions intended for distant audiences. However, in comparison to Evaristo, he produced less
language across the four English tasks.

> Oral picture description to a present audience: About the kids, how they try
> to get lambs. This one's got one out and they're trying to get 'em. Like he
> jumped over here and they're trying to put it back where he belongs. And
> the kid has food on his hands to see if the lamb will come to him and he'll
> pick him up and go outside. That's all.

Although Oscar attempted, in the first picture description, to introduce the description by opening with "[It's] about the kids, how they try
to get lambs," his introduction was somewhat overly general and gave
no indication of the number of kids or the setting in which the action
took place. His use of pronouns was also similarly ambiguous and appeared to presuppose shared knowledge between interlocutors. For example, Oscar explained that "this *one's* got *one* out and they're trying to
get 'em," but it was unclear just who got whom and to whom "they" and
"them" referred. His assumption of shared knowledge was evident in his
next statement, in which he emphasized "over here" but verbally specified the location he was referring to: "Like he jumped *over here* and
they're trying to put *it* back where *he* belongs." Finally, he concluded his
description by stating to the listener, "That's all." When we examine his
description closely, it appears as if Oscar's *oral* picture descriptions ex-

hibit a shopping-list quality. On the oral descriptions, Oscar did not employ clear introductory sentences to frame the rest of his description. Instead, his general strategy was to introduce characters one at a time and to utilize large numbers of color descriptors to describe clothing and objects present in the illustration.

> Oral picture description to a distant audience: There's a man. He's rolling a ball. There's two kids cheering. There's two, there's six things [pins] and the man's trying to roll the ball to hit it. And he has a black ball, yellow pants, and a blue sweatshirt and white tennis shoes. And then the boy, he has blond hair. And he has blue pants and he has white tennis shoes. And he is clappin' his hands. There's the girl, she has blue tennis shoes. She has pink pants and she has a different colored shirt. And she has brown hair. And the floor is yellow. In front of the six things, the six sticks that are standing up, on top of there is a heart and six little boxes: three on one side and three on the other. And that's all.

Interestingly, in the oral description to a distant audience, Oscar did not employ an introductory sentence. He did not appear to preplan his description; instead, he listed characters one by one and then proceeded to describe each on the basis of clothing color and color of physical features, such as eye and hair color. For example, in the third sentence, he mentioned that two kids were cheering, and then two sentences later, he remarked, "And then the boy, he has blond hair. And he has blue pants and he has white tennis shoes." It appears as if Oscar equated greater explicitness and clarity with the production of greater amounts of language. On this task, Oscar again concluded his description with "That's it."

Both of Oscar's written picture descriptions differed from the two oral picture descriptions. He produced slightly less language and fewer color descriptors on the written picture descriptions, and yet, he utilized more introductory sentences.

> Written picture description to a present audience: One day four girls and one baby went to pick rocks in the pond. They put their hats and pail next to the big rock. All the girls wore dresses and one of the girls was standing up looking at her purse that was filled with rocks. After that, the girls went home to show their mom the rocks from the pond.

On his written description to a present audience, Oscar introduced his description in this way: "One day four girls and one baby went to pick rocks in the pond." In this sentence, Oscar specified the number of characters and the particular setting (although he did so incorrectly because the illustration depicts a beach and not a pond).

Similarly, on the written description to a distant audience, Oscar utilized an introductory sentence in order to render the description overtly explicit. He opened, "One day the mother pig was making breakfast for her sons and daughters." Then he quickly added, by way of clarification regarding the number of characters, "And she had *five* pigs." He did not, however, make the setting explicit.

> Written picture description to a distant audience: One day the mother pig was making breakfast for her sons and daughters. And she had five pigs. One of the pigs was taking the dishes to the living room for breakfast. And one of the girl pigs dropped one of her mom's favorite glasses. And the pigs' names are Amy, Pat, Joe, Sam, and Sue. And one of the pigs was making strawberry jam on his bread for lunch.

After introducing the picture, Oscar went on to describe some of the action taking place but did so in a shopping-list manner. He seemed to be scanning the picture and describing whatever character or action happened to catch his eye. He did not explicitly conclude his description as he had done on the oral tasks, and he stopped after the last sentence, "And one of the pigs was making strawberry jam on his bread for lunch."

It was not altogether clear why Oscar relied on a greater production of color descriptors to render his oral descriptions more explicit and why he did not employ a similar strategy on the written tasks. Instead, on the written tasks, he consistently employed more explicit introductory sentences to render his descriptions clearer to the audience.

As discussed earlier in this chapter, the students demonstrated reliance on similar linguistic contextualizing strategies on the Spanish picture description tasks. However, despite similarities in general strategy, one interesting language difference emerged: The lower-achieving students tended to produce more language on the Spanish tasks than did their higher-achieving peers. It is quite possible that, despite language proficiency test results, students identified as lower achieving are more proficient in Spanish than their peers identified as higher achieving.

The third student language sample consists of Marissa Nava's four picture descriptions. I selected her language samples to illustrate the general linguistic contextualizing strategies demonstrated by most of the children, regardless of ability group designation.

Marissa Nava—High-Achieving Student.   Marissa's primary linguistically contextualized strategy, across tasks, consisted of producing more language in an effort to render her picture descriptions overtly specific and explicit. Across ability groups and similar to their performance on the four English picture description tasks, the target students produced the greatest amount of language on the oral linguistically contextualized task. Marissa's oral picture description directed to a present audience was considerably briefer than her oral picture description directed at a distant audience. The word in italics represents a code-switch into English.

> Oral picture description to a present audience: Unas niñas están jugando a la pelota. El papá está cortando el zacate. El más chiquito está volando un papalote. La niña está brincando y haciendo maromas. Los otros dos niños—uno está en la calle y otro está en el zacate y estan jugando a la pelota. El perro quiere agarrar una ardilla que está en el árbol. Su mamá está cortando las plantas. Hay una casa grande. Hay una troca como donde meten *furniture*. Tiene colores, está toda anaranjada. Tiene colores verde, amarillo, y rosa. La mamá es güera.
>
> (Some little girls are playing ball. The father is cutting the grass. The smallest one is flying a kite. The little girl is jumping and doing somersaults. The other two children—one is in the street and the other is on the grass and is playing ball. The dog wants to catch a squirrel that is in the tree. Their mother is cutting plants. There is a large house. There is a truck where they put furniture. It has many colors, it is all orange. It has green, yellow, and pink. The mother is blond.)

In this picture description, Marissa did not utilize an introductory sentence to introduce either the setting or the characters present in the picture. Instead, similar to Evaristo and Oscar, she described each character or set of characters one by one in an almost shopping-list fashion. She began by stating that "some little girls are playing ball." (In reality, the picture depicts the family lawn, where six family members and their dog are engaged in a variety of activities. In this picture, two boys are playing ball while one boy flies a kite, their sister runs, and their parents engage in yardwork.) Marissa then explained that the father was cutting the grass.

In the third sentence, she explained that "el más chiquito está volando un papalote" (the smallest one [a boy] is flying a kite), but it was unclear which boy she was describing since she had previously mentioned only "some little girls" and "the father." After mentioning the "smallest boy," she described "the little girl who is jumping and doing somersaults." Her use of "*the* little girl," again, was ambiguous since the only girls she had previously described were "some little girls," so it is not entirely clear to whom Marissa was referring. The rest of the picture description consisted of listing characters or objects, including the "two other [male] children," the dog, the mother, the house, and the truck.

Marissa employed a few locatives and clarificatory markers in her description. For example, when describing the two [male] children, she specified that "one is *in the street* and the other is *on the grass*." When describing the squirrel that the dog wanted to catch, she specified "a squirrel that is *in the tree*." When she attempted to describe the moving van in the illustration, she specified "a truck *where they put furniture*." It is also interesting to note that the student code-switched once when she employs the English word *furniture* to specify the type of truck she was describing. She also used the nonstandard Spanish anglicized term *troca* for *truck* instead of the standard *camioneta.*

Finally, Marissa did not end her description explicitly; instead, she concluded by stating that the illustration had many colors and listing some: orange, green, yellow, and pink. Finally, she stated that "the mother is blond." Despite some use of locatives and clarificatory markers, in general Marissa produced a description that could not be understood without access to the illustration, which is understandable given that the task is meant for a present audience.

It is evident, on the next task—the oral description meant for a distant audience—that Marissa attempted to render this description clearer and more overtly explicit. She did so by producing more language on this task in comparison to the previous task and by mentioning details such as the color of the characters' clothing and other objects present in the illustration. In addition, she employed more locatives and clarificatory markers. Interestingly, she also code-switched more often (code-switches are in italics for easy identification).

Oral picture description to a distant audience: Una familia quiere hacer una casita chiquita. Un niño está clavando los *nails* y otro niño está cortando la madera con el serrucho. Y otro niño está sentado como en una caja de madera y está mirando el plan. El más chiquito está arriba de la caja para [?] el serrucho. Otro también está arriba de la caja para—con el—está usando el martillo. Hay una caja de *nails*. Hay un desarmador. El niño que está sentando tiene una camiseta morada, pantalones negros con *Converse—the shoes Converse.* Y tiene cabello café. Se está riendo. Tiene los ojos chiquitos y el otro niño tiene *Converse* también. Tiene pantalones azules y una camiseta anaranjada. Tiene cabello café y está en una caja también. Y el otro niño que está también en una caja. Tiene pantalones azules con una camiseta blanca y cabello café con rojo. Y tiene un martillo en la mano. Y abajo hay un bote de pintura. El bote es rojo. La pintura es blanca. Hay un cepillo de pintar—rojo con anaranjado. Hay madera y hay otro martillo. Y hay un desarmador rojo. Y estan en una mesa donde cortan cosas. Y tiene un patio. Atrás de ellos hay un patio. Su papá está recogiendo la madera. Su papá tiene unos zapatos tennis. Tiene pantalones gris. Tiene camiseta verde. Tiene madera y tiene cabello café. Y el patio es amarillo y hay como una cama allí. Hay una silla. Los dos son amarillos. Hay la mesa que es amarilla y lo . . . como el paragüas que tienen ellos es amarillo con rojo. Y la casa de ellos es verde con blanca. Y una ventana tiene *shutters.* Tienen como los que usan para las *stamps.* Bueno, a éso se parecen. Hay en el zacate muchos arboles. Hay una cazuela a un lado. Un lado de la casa que tienen ellos. Y hay un cerco de *brick.* Es anaranjado.

(A family wants to build a small house. A little boy is hammering the nails and another boy is sawing wood with a saw. And another boy is sitting on something like a wooden box and is looking at the plan. The smallest one is on top of the box to [?] the saw. Another is also on top of the box to—with the—he is using the hammer. There is a box of nails. There is a screwdriver. The boy that is sitting on the box has a purple t-shirt, black pants with "Converse"—the shoes "Converse." And he has brown hair. He is laughing. He has small eyes and the other boy has "Converse" too. He has blue pants and an orange t-shirt. He has brown hair and he is on a box too. And the other boy is also on a box. He has blue pants and a white t-shirt and brownish-reddish hair. And he has a hammer in his hand. And, below there is a bucket of paint. The bucket is red and the paint is white. There is a paint brush—red with yellows. There is wood and there is another hammer. And there is a red screwdriver. And they are next to a table that is used for cutting things. And they have a patio, the patio is behind them. Their father is picking up wood. Their father has tennis shoes. He has gray pants. He has a green t-shirt. He has wood and brown hair. And the patio is yellow, and there is like a bed there. There is a chair. The two are yellows with red. And their house is green with white. And one of the windows has shutters. They have something, like what's used with stamps. They resemble those. And on the grass there are many trees. There is a pot on one side, on one side of the house that belongs to them. And there is a fence made of brick. It is orange.)

Marissa began her description by introducing the illustration, "A family wants to build a small house." Then she went on to describe, in shopping-list fashion, the various characters and their actions ("a little boy is hammering the nails," "another boy is sawing wood with a saw," "there is a screwdriver," "the bucket is red and the paint is white," "their father has tennis shoes," "he has gray pants. He has a green t-shirt").

Her focus on colors and other detail is evident. She described the colors of t-shirts and pants. Sometimes, the focus on color was distracting because the listener had no way of knowing what sources of information needed to be backgrounded and which needed to be foregrounded. For example, she said, "And, below there is a bucket of paint. The bucket is red and the paint is white. There is a paint brush—red with yellow . . . And there is a red screwdriver." It is also interesting to note that Marissa code-switched a total of four times on this task. She employed the English words *nails, shutters, stamps,* and *brick* instead of the Spanish terms *clavos, postigo, estampillas* or *timbres,* and *ladrillo.* Marissa also employed the English brand name *Converse* to specify the types of shoes the boys in the illustration were wearing.

Despite her tendency to describe using an almost shopping-list approach, Marissa employed a greater number of clarificatory markers and locatives in this description in comparison to the contextualized version shared earlier. For example, she specified that the boy she was describing "*is sitting on the box*" and that "the other boy is also *on a box.*" She also explained that the hammer she was describing "is *in his [the boy's] hand.*" Marissa also made explicit that the boys she was describing "are *next to a table* that is used for cutting things" and that "the patio is *behind them.*"

Despite the greater use of locatives and clarificatory markers, Marissa did not appear to preplan her description in order to render it overly explicit and precise; the shopping-list quality, combined with the distracting focus on color, yielded the opposite result: a somewhat unwieldy and unclear description.

In contrast to her extensive oral language production, Marissa's written picture descriptions were brief, as the next two samples show. Her introductory sentence on the contextualized task was overly general: "This picture has to do with a [female] duck," and Marissa did not elaborate sufficiently in order to produce a coherent description. She produced a description that was brief and one that very much required that the listener have access to the illustration in order to imagine it.

> Written picture description to a present audience: Esta foto se trata de una pata. Ella está bañando a sus niños. Dos de ellos estan agarrando una toalla. Uno de ellos tiró la agua. Su papá está arreglando [?]. Su papá tiene frio. Por éso carga una bolsa de agua caliente y galletas.
>
> (This picture has to do with a [female] duck. She is bathing her children. Two of them are holding a towel. One of them spilled water. Their father is fixing [?]. Their father is cold. That is why he carries a hot water bottle and cookies.)

Marissa's written picture description, meant for a distant reader, was quite similar to the one directed to a present audience. The description was brief, and she relied on details such as the color of items (the pants, the car, the cushions, the tires, and the cat) to render them overtly explicit. In addition to color descriptors, Marissa also employed more specific adjectives, such as *antique* cars and *sailor's* cap.

> Written picture description to a distant audience: Lo que está pasando en esta foto son dos osos con ropa. Estan arreglando un carro. El carro es como del día de los carros antiguos. El oso tiene una gorra de marinero. Un oso de pantalones verdes está abajo del carro. El otro se machucó con el desarmador. El carro es rojo con verde colchones. Tiene llantas blancas. Tiene un gato negro arriba.
>
> (What is happening in this picture are two bears with clothes. They are fixing a car. The car is like from the days of antique cars. The bear has a sailor's cap. The bear with green pants is under the car. The other hurt himself with the screwdriver. The car is red with green cushions. It has white tires. It has a black cat on top of it.)

Marissa produced less language on this written task in comparison to her oral language production. Although she attempted to introduce the illustration, she did so in an overly general manner: "What is happening in this picture are two bears with clothes." Interestingly and in contrast to her oral descriptions, Marissa did not code-switch on either of the written descriptions, regardless of differing audience needs.

It is evident from the student picture descriptions presented here that, across tasks, the students responded differently to tasks that called for communicating with distant audiences than those that did not. The students responded to these linguistic demands by producing more language on tasks that required greater explicitness and clarity, as opposed to those allowing for a greater presumption of shared knowledge between the speaker or writer and audience. However, as can be discerned from the examples cited earlier, the children's descriptions often resembled shopping lists and had a great focus on slightly irrelevant details, such as an overemphasis on the color of items in the pictures.

The picture description results clearly show that the students produced more language, describing words, and introductory narrative strategies on the picture description tasks requiring them to communicate with distant listeners and readers. When the students were asked to describe pictures to viable distant audiences, they attempted, across achievement groups, to modify their language to produce what they considered to be more comprehensible descriptions. The students demonstrated a greater ability to linguistically contextualize their language orally than in written fashion. When the language tasks did not require them to communicate with believable distant audiences, they relied on assumed shared knowledge (such as listener or reader access to the pictures), as on the picture description tasks and the noun definition tasks. This will be discussed in the section that follows.

Noun Definition Tasks

The noun definition tasks used ten words identical to those on the WISC-R vocabulary subtests. Students were asked to define the words *knife, umbrella, clock, hat, bicycle, nail, alphabet, donkey, thief,* and *diamond.* (Spanish equivalents are *cuchillo, paraguas (sombrilla), reloj, sombrero, bicicleta, clavo, alfabeto (abecedario), burro, ladrón,* and *diamante.*) The purpose of these tasks was to gauge whether and how students modified their language when asked to define the nouns in English and in Spanish to an imaginary distant audience. The procedure included giving the student a word and asking him or her to define the word in a way that would allow a peer not present to understand the significance of the word.

During analysis, I identified the definitions produced as either formal and linguistically contextualized or as informal. Basically, I analyzed the target students' definitions for the presence or absence of formal defining syntax. Linguistically contextualized or formal definitions were identified as following a particular syntactic form and requiring a statement of class membership followed by a specification of the proper subset of the class (such as "x" is [superordinate term] that [relative clause]). For example, the definition " a car is a vehicle that travels on four wheels" represents a linguistically contextualized definition in that the referent, "a car," is subsumed by the superordinate "vehicle," and the relative clause provides additional information that is specific and correct in regard to the referent.[6]

More contextualized or informal ways of communicating the meaning of a referent include using examples, synonyms, or descriptions of the referent's features or functions in place of the formal defining syntax. The absence of the formal syntax suggests that the speaker presumes some knowledge about the referent on the part of the listener (for example, knife—"you use it for cutting stuff," whereby the speaker assumes the listener knows that a knife is a sharp object and is aware of the type of "stuff" a knife cuts and slices).

Results from the noun definition tasks confirmed that when a language task did not explicitly require the students to communicate with a believable distant audience, they responded by assuming shared background knowledge with the listener. As a result, they employed more informal definition strategies on the noun definition tasks. This tendency was indicated by the production of definitions lacking the formal syntax necessary to render them linguistically contextualized.

Student Preference for Informal Definitions

English Definition Task. The majority of students produced more informal definitions than formal or linguistically contextualized ones. On the English task, approximately 78 percent of the definitions produced by all the students lacked the necessary formal syntactical form (see Figure 5.3). Only 22 percent of the definitions produced were identified as linguistically contextualized, or formal, definitions. There appeared to be little difference between achievement groups. Eighty percent of the higher achievers' definitions and 77 percent of the lower achievers' definitions were categorized as contextualized.

The following examples illustrate the target students' tendency to produce definitions lacking the linguistically contextualized or formal definition genre. These definitions suggest that students assumed some degree of shared background knowledge with listeners.

Informal or contextualized definitions of the word *clock*:

"Something that does 'tick-tock' everyday." (Oscar)
"Something that tell you the time." (Felice)

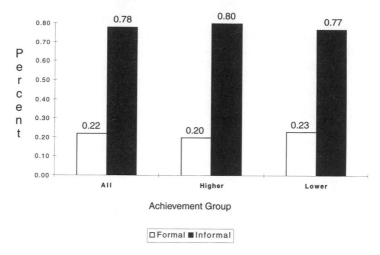

FIGURE 5.3 *English Definitions: Preferred Type by Achievement Group*

"It goes 'tick-tock' and it tells you the time." (Joey)
"A clock shows the time." (Raquel)
"A clock helps you tell the time. You could hang it up or wear it
   around your wrist. It's round and different colors." (Miguel)
"Clock. To see the time or to wake you up in the morning." (Blanca)

Formal or linguistically contextualized definitions of the word *clock*:

"A clock is something that tells time, like if you have an appointment
   and you don't know if you're late or if you're early, you just look at
   the clock. Or if you want to watch your favorite program on television, you just look at the clock 'cause you have to know what
   time it comes on." (Marissa)
"It is a device that tells you the time you can bring along if you have
   a wristwatch." (Evaristo)

Spanish Definition Task.   The language of the task did not appear to affect the students' production of informal definitions. The majority of all
the students' Spanish definitions, approximately 78 percent, were similarly informal or contextualized (see Figure 5.4).
   The following examples illustrate the target students' similar tendency to produce Spanish definitions lacking the linguistically contextualized or formal definition genre.
   Informal or contextualized definitions of the word *reloj* (clock):

"Se usan para saber el tiempo." (They're worn to tell time.) (Miguel)

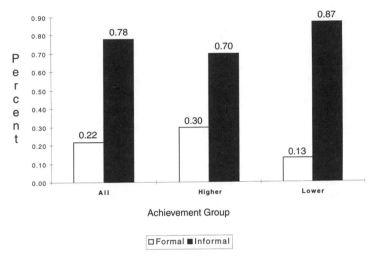

FIGURE 5.4   *Spanish Definitions: Preferred Type by Achievement Group*

"Dice la hora y la minutos y la segundos, 'seconds.' Si puedes lle-
varlo en tu mano." (It tells the hour and the minutes and the seconds. And you can wear it on your hand.) (Evaristo)

"Te dice la hora." (It tells you the time.) (Raquel)

"Te dice el tiempo. Tiene 'hands' y es 'electrical.'" (It tells the time. It
has hands and it's electrical.) (Joey)

"Te dice la hora, te despierta en la mañana. Está redondo o
cuadrado. A veces son blancos o negros. Estan chiquitos or
grandotes. Se pone en la mano. Tiene números. Da vueltas el pal-
ito chiquito." (It tells the time, it wakes you up in the morning. It
is round or square. Sometimes they are white or black. They are
small and big. They're worn on the wrist. It has numbers. The
small hand goes around.) (Raquel)

"Algo que miras el tiempo o para saber cuando vas a ir a un lugar. Y te
lo poner en el brazo. Está chiquito. Tiene manitas, tiene números.
Tiene como un 'tape' para te lo puedas poner." (Something you
look at to tell time or to know when you have to go somewhere.
And you put it on your wrist. It's small. It has little hands and numbers. It has something like tape so you can put it on.) (Blanca)

"Algo que te dice las horas y los días [?]. Y tiene muchos números. Y
dice la hora." (Something that tells you the hours and the days
[?]. And it has many numbers. And it tells the time.) (Oscar)

Contrary to earlier findings showing the lower-achieving students were more proficient in Spanish, the higher achievers produced
slightly more Spanish formal definitions on this task than did the lower

achievers. Thirty percent of the Spanish definitions produced by the higher-achieving group and 13 percent of the lower-achieving group's Spanish definitions were identified as linguistically contextualized. However, the general trend remained the same: The students relied more heavily on informal or contextualized language strategies when defining referents verbally.

This trend suggests that the students may not have been aware of the degree of explicitness required of them on this particular task to make the referent's meaning clear to an imaginary distant listener. It is also possible that the students may not have known how to modify their language in such a situation. A third possibility may be that the students were not aware of the importance of utilizing this syntactical form; since most of the students produced at least one formal definition, they demonstrated that they could produce the form, but they did not do so consistently.

Types of Linguistically Contextualized Definitions Produced: Not Entirely Appropriate

When I examined the features of the formal or linguistically contextualized definitions produced, I found that, in spite of the fact that the students produced *some* formal or linguistically contextualized definitions, the strategies employed were not entirely appropriate. The two achievement groups behaved in linguistically similar ways on the definition tasks, regardless of the language of the task, although the higher-achieving group received slightly higher specificity scores on the superordinates produced, as well as higher scores on semantic effectiveness on the relative clauses.

Specificity of Superordinates. Across languages and achievement groups, the students generally scored within the 2.0 to 2.5 range for their superordinate scores, indicating that their production of linguistically contextualized definitions tended to utilize overly generalized superordinates, such as *thing* (*una cosa*), *something* (*algo*), or *someone* (*alguien*) (see Table 5.1).

On the English definition task, the higher-achieving group scored slightly higher on production of superordinates. The higher achievers received a mean average score of 2.40, and the lower achievement group averaged 1.95. The results indicate that students from both achievement groups tended to incorporate overly generalized superordinates into their linguistically contextualized definitions.

On the Spanish definition task, both achievement groups continued to score similarly. The higher-achieving group received a mean average

TABLE 5.1 [Super-ordinate] Use in Formal Definitions

	English	*Spanish*
All students		
Average	2.10	2.25
(SD)	0.35	0.88
Higher-achieving group		
Average	2.40	2.50
(SD)	0.57	0.87
Lower-achieving group		
Average	1.95	2.00
(SD)	0.10	1.00

SD = Standard Deviation

specificity score of 2.50, and the lower-achieving group scored 2.0. Again, students from both achievement groups employed somewhat overly generalized superordinates in their formal definitions.

The following are examples of the types of formal definitions and overly general superordinates produced by the students: *Ladrón (Thief)*—"Un ladrón es *alguien* que le gusta robar cosas como dinero" (*A thief is someone that likes to steal things like money*) (Marissa); *Clock*—"A clock is *something* that tells time" (Evaristo).

Most often, the students relied on overly general superordinates that were not specific enough to be considered appropriate.

Relative Clause Features.   The students' tendency to incorporate vague and overly general features into their linguistically contextualized definitions also became apparent when the appropriateness of their relative clauses was examined. Across languages, the students' semantic appropriateness scores for their relative clauses ranged from a low of 2.0 to a high of 2.37 (see Table 5.2).

On the English definition task, students from both achievement groups again performed similarly; the higher-achieving group scored a mean average of 2.37, and the lower-achieving group scored 2.15. These scores indicate the use of helpful and correct but overly general relative clauses.

On the Spanish definition task, the characteristics of the students' relative clauses were also overly general. Students from the higher achievement group received a slightly higher mean average score than those from the lower achieving group; the higher achievers averaged 2.15, and the lower achievers 2.0. Both scores again indicate student reliance on relative clauses that are overly general and not entirely precise.

The following formal or linguistically contextualized definitions contain examples of the type of overly general relative clause most fre-

TABLE 5.2   Relative Clause Use on Formal Definitions

	English	Spanish
All students		
Average	2.22	2.07
(SD)	0.79	0.73
Higher-achieving group		
Average	2.37	2.15
(SD)	0.05	1.03
Lower-achieving group		
Average	2.15	2.00
(SD)	1.01	0.50

SD = Standard Deviation

quently employed by the target students: *Diamond*—"It's something *that you put on your earrings*" (Felice); *Hat*—"A hat is something *that people wear when it's hot or just for fun*" (Marissa).

The students incorporated overly general relative clauses into their formal definitions. The clauses did not directly reflect the noun being defined; rather, they could refer to a number of referents. In addition, while ignoring the referents' features, students focused on the functional attributes of the words being defined. The students' focus on functional attributes also appeared in their informal definitions. This defining strategy will be discussed at greater depth in the following section on informal or contextualized definition characteristics.

In general, across achievement groups, the students produced few formal or linguistically contextualized definitions. And when they did produce formal definitions, they incorporated superordinates and relative clauses categorized as overly general and vague. As a result, even though the students did produce the formal syntactical form necessary to render linguistically contextualized definitions, the linguistic cues they employed did not yield clear and precise definitions. So, although the students employed the correct syntactical form, their use of overly general linguistic strategies suggests that they perceived the listener as an immediate audience rather than a distant one and relied on perceived shared background knowledge when defining the nouns.

Preferred Informal Definition Strategies

As discussed, the students relied heavily on informal strategies when defining words in both English and Spanish. When these definitions were examined, three strategies were found to be used frequently by the students, across languages and achievement groups, to convey the meaning of the referents.

The students' three preferred strategies across languages were (1) descriptive features, (2) examples, and (3) functional statements. *Descriptive features* refer to those features that are correct but are not included on a list of conventional features normally associated with the word being defined. (For example, "sharp" and "pointy" are adjectives conventionally attributed to *knife*.) Descriptive features in this study are features the students attributed to the noun. *Examples* are noun phrases that present a concrete, specific situation correctly related to the referent's application of a particular object. *Functional statements* define the purpose or action of the noun being described (for example, "a knife is used for cutting"). Functional statements were also counted as examples (for instance, "a hat is something you wear on your head when you go to a concert").

The students regularly employed definitional strategies that required listener knowledge or shared knowledge for the definition to be meaningful. The students' use of strategies such as descriptive features presupposed a referential background shared with the listener because the descriptive features provided by the students were not conventional and not normally associated with the word being defined (for example, using "gray" to describe the noun *nail*).

The students' reliance on examples and functional statements also signaled their presumption of referential background shared with the audience. By providing the audience with examples and functional statements, the speaker overlooks the basic need to describe the referent using customary and orthodox features; instead, he or she assumes shared knowledge concerning those features, then jumps ahead to describe the functions and provide examples regarding the nouns being defined.

This tendency was evident in the majority of the students' informal definitions that contained descriptive feature. On the English definition task, 76 percent of the definitions produced by all students contained descriptive features. The students from the higher-achieving group employed descriptive features slightly more often than their lower-achieving peers in this task—88 percent and 63 percent, respectively.

In addition to relying on nonconventional features, the students consistently "padded" their definitions with examples. Across achievement groups, 58 percent of the English definitions and 77 percent of the Spanish definitions contained examples. Examples occurred regularly on both the English and Spanish tasks. However, both groups of students relied slightly more on the use of examples on the Spanish tasks. Sixty percent of the higher achievers' contextualized English definitions included examples, as did 57 percent of the lower achievers' definitions. Conversely, of the contextualized Spanish definitions produced by the higher-achieving group, 75 percent incorporated examples, as did 79 percent of the contextualized Spanish definitions of the lower-achieving group.

The third most frequently employed informal contextualizing strategy consisted of functional statements. In addition, the examples cited by the students often reflected some functional aspect of the referent. The students demonstrated the inclination to utilize functional statements in their informal or contextualized definitions; 76 percent of the English definitions and 79 percent of the Spanish definitions contained a functional statement. Both achievement groups scored similarly on these tasks; however, the higher achievers utilized a slightly greater percentage of functional statements on the English definitions, and the lower achievers produced more functional statements on the Spanish definitions task. Eighty-one percent of the higher group's and 70 percent of the lower group's contextualized English definitions contained functional statements. In addition, 67 percent of the higher group's and 88 percent of the lower group's Spanish definitions incorporated functional statements of some type.

Some examples of definitions that included functional statements follow: *Diamond*—"and diamonds can be worn as jewelry—on your neck, on your wrist, or just for decoration and most of the rich peoples always have diamonds" (Evaristo); *Sombrero (Hat)*—"Es algo que te pones cuando hace mucho sol" (It is something that you wear when it is sunny) (Raquel).

In addition to being coded for frequency of use, functional statements were also coded for specificity. Specificity results suggest that, across achievement groups, the students produced functional statements that were somewhat general and not specific enough to define the referents accurately. The scoring format for specificity was as follows: 0 indicated no use of functional statements, 1 indicated use of a vague functional statement, and 2 indicated an appropriate statement of function. The students' average specificity score was 1.25 on the English contextualized definition task (see Table 5.3).

The scores indicate that the students' functional statements were vague—either overly general or too restricted to be considered entirely appropriate and correct. The average specificity scores assigned to the functional statements were similar across achievement groups. The higher-achieving group scored 1.10 on the English definition task and .94 on the Spanish definition task. The lower-achieving group scored 1.20 and 1.35 on the same tasks, respectively. The results show that all the students employed functional statements that were not specific enough to the nouns being defined. For example, Evaristo's definition of a diamond stated that it "can be worn as jewelry," and Raquel explained

TABLE 5.3   Specificity/Appropriateness Scores of Functional Statements

	English	Spanish
All	1.25	1.00
Higher group	1.10	0.94
Lower group	1.20	1.35

Key: 0—none
       1—vague
       2—correct

that a hat is "something that you wear when it's sunny." Although both of these functional statements are true and applicable to the nouns being defined, the functions presented are not confined to the referents: A variety of objects can be worn as jewelry or when it is sunny.

Few differences in frequency of formal definition production across students were observed. The majority of the students produced both informal and formal definitions in both languages, but they consistently produced a greater number of informal definitions. In addition, because the students were able to produce some formal definitions, they demonstrated their ability to construct the appropriate syntactical form. However, they appeared to be unaware that the ability to produce such syntactical forms is valued since they did not do so consistently.

The students relied on similar informal contextualizing language strategies to convey the meaning of the referent to the distant audience. The students employed descriptive features, examples, and functional statements consistently in their informal definitions across languages. Few significant differences between achievement groups were discerned for this task. Essentially, the achievement groups performed in ways that were indistinguishable from each other.

The students' reliance on informal contextualizing language strategies may have been influenced by the context in which the task was administered. Because the words being defined were quite basic, the students may have assumed an understanding shared with the listener regarding the referent meanings. Even though the students were asked to define each word for a physically distant audience, it is plausible that they did not perceive the listener as truly distant. Consequently, they treated the audience as a physically present entity with whom noun meanings could be communicated through more contextualized strategies.

The facility of the task may also have contributed to the students' greater reliance on informal contextualized strategies. The ten words defined in the task are basic concrete nouns, and the students may have had difficulty assuming that the audience had little knowledge of the words. This assumption of shared knowledge may have contributed to the students' focusing on functional attributes and overly general descriptive features instead of relying on conventional features that would describe the referent itself. The students appeared to assume that the audience was familiar with the basic physical characteristics of the items being defined. Therefore, they may have proceeded to provide the audience with a secondary layer of information, referring to the uses of the nouns and giving examples of those uses.

It appears that when the concept of the distant audience was not believable, the students assumed shared knowledge, and their use of informal contextualizing defining strategies reflected their assumptions of that shared knowledge. In addition, the strictly verbal nature of the definition task may have affected the students' responses. Unlike the picture description task, the noun definition task did not present variance in context. On the picture description task, the students were asked to define pictures under four conditions, varying in language mode; they were asked to describe these pictures verbally and in written form. The task also varied in terms of audience language demands. During the task, the students were asked to describe the pictures to a physically present listener and to a viably distant listener. Under these conditions, which explicitly required the students to produce clear and unambiguous messages, they responded by modifying their language use to communicate more effectively with the distant audience. The students were better able to produce linguistically contextualized language on both oral picture description tasks. This finding suggests that the students (1) were better able to linguistically contextualize via the oral mode, and (2) recognized that the linguistically contextualized tasks required greater explicitness and clarity on their part. It is unfortunate that this nascent communicative competence was not recognized and built on in class.

6 Rethinking Academic Discourses: Some Pedagogical Comments

As the preceding chapters indicate, I adopted a critical sociocultural framework in this research that allowed for a broader perspective of literacy, beyond a focus on minimal levels of reading and writing ability as indicators of literacy skills. Literacy is not defined as merely the ability to read and write; it is also a culturally prescribed way of using both oral and written language. The ability to produce literate discourses (as judged by traditional measures of academic performance) is a result of formal and/or informal language socialization practices in mainstream institutions such as schools and middle-class families. Individuals acquire literacy skills through the exercise of culture-specific practices. Thus, as Paulo Freire has often suggested, an "educational practice should never be restricted to a 'reading of the word,' a 'reading of text,' but rather . . . it should also include a 'reading of context,' a 'reading of the world.'"[1] For this reason, the reading of academic discourses cannot be divorced from the middle-class white context that informs it. Therefore, an educational practice that purports to teach academic discourses to linguistic-minority students from working-class backgrounds must, first and foremost, critically socialize these students in ways that enable them to make sense of the middle-class white world that often serves as a point of reference for meaning-making in academic discourses. That is, working-class linguistic-minority students must be helped to gain membership in the middle-class world of the academic discourses if they are going to successfully and critically appropriate those discourses.

A critical sociocultural view recognizes that the language skills that result from mainstream practices are not inherently superior to skills that result from nonmainstream practices. Thus, a critical sociocultural view of language and literacy promotes objective examination of literate discourse patterns in different cultures and avoids ethnocentricity and negative judgments about the value of specific language skills that result from such patterns.

A critical sociocultural perspective of language and literacy assisted me in developing a framework for examining both student academic language use and the role of the audience (teachers and peers) on eliciting student linguistically contextualized language. Through this perspective, I was able to avoid a deficit approach to examining the ways working-class Mexican American students produced language so as to make meaning in different contexts. Instead of viewing language skills as static, that is, as either existing or not existing, a critical sociocultural framework alternates between language skills that individuals exhibit and the context or contexts in which the individuals are expected to function. This dual focus allowed me to examine the effects of context on student use of linguistically contextualized language.

Although my analysis focused on bilingual Mexican American students, many of the patterns that emerged could also be characteristic of other linguistic-minority students who struggle to make sense of the often competing and conflicting linguistic worlds within which they exist. The academic underachievement of Mexican Americans is a well-recognized and well-documented phenomenon. Historically, the group's academic underachievement has been attributed to a lack of English proficiency. Little, however, has been documented regarding the academic language demands that English proficient bilingual Mexican American students contend with in school contexts.

As the discussion of the language tasks results indicates, the Mexican American students I observed produced linguistically contextualized language in response to those tasks that explicitly required them to communicate with distant audiences. This suggests that working-class linguistic-minority students are able to discourse code-switch if the classroom pedagogy provides the linguistic and cultural context necessary for code-switching to occur. What also became clear is that if the teaching of the academic discourses is effective (to the extent that it creates conditions leading to access to the middle-class white cultural values that shape and sustain the teaching of academic discourse), linguistic-minority students will succeed in appropriating that discourse.

The results also suggest that, across language tasks, students modified their language use when addressing believable distant audiences. "Believable," in this case, refers to a speaker-listener context to which these students could relate. Simply put, in contexts where it was clear that they were expected to share information with a physically absent listener or reader, the students incorporated a greater number of features of what has been referred to in the literature as "*de*-contextualized" language into their discourse. Unfortunately, the students did not rely solely on what are considered conventional academic features for such "*de*-contextualization." The inability to linguistically contextualize in more academic ways suggests that the students were not given access to the cultural and academic contexts in which a particular language event will meaningfully communicate a speaker's intent.

For this reason, I stressed in previous chapters that the teaching of academic discourse requires that teachers critically socialize their students in ways of being in the middle-class world so that they can begin to critically use the cultural capital that informs and sustains a middle-class white reality. Without entry into that reality, which serves as a base for academic discourses, it is, on the one hand, impossible to effectively teach academic discourses; on the other hand, it would be preposterous for teachers to expect linguistic-minority and other minority students, including working-class whites, to pull academic discourses out of a hat and magically and effectively use it across class and cultural boundaries.

The language tasks results also support François Jacob's claim that all human beings are born programmed to learn,[2] to the extent that these students produced a great amount of language that was guided by the more effective teaching of their immediate sociocultural context rather than the artificial and often inconsistent teaching of the classroom that (perhaps unknowingly) produced a disarticulation between students' language, culture, and context. For the learning of academic discourse to occur, teachers not only must accept Jacob's premise that we are all born programmed to learn but also must find pedagogical ways that are psychologically harmless and that enhance students' epistemological curiosity. Thus, the explicit teaching about the often hidden values and assumptions of the middle-class white reality that guides the meaning-making process in that reality must be part of any effective teaching that expects linguistic-minority and other minority students to acquire academic communicative competence.

The language tasks results also showed that the teacher did not tap the linguistic resources that the students brought into the classroom. Even though Amy Cortland expected her students to use language in more conventional academic ways, the students demonstrated greater ease in using an oral mode (which is more prevalent in their sociocultural context) to linguistically contextualize their language. For example, all students produced a greater number of t-units and narrative strategies on both the English and Spanish oral linguistically contextualized tasks. Unfortunately, the teacher was not able to tap this strength and further develop their oral language skills, which are, incidentally, the bedrock of all written discourse.

In other words, oral language capacities always precede their written forms. As Paulo Freire eloquently pointed out, men and women did not develop their language by writing first. Thus, historically, writing represents a later stage in the development of human communication. However, the teacher in this study, for a variety of reasons, was not able to engage students in a developmental process of orality, wherein the students' oral home language (their primary discourse) served as a base for more academic oral language development—a prerequisite for reading and writing. The teacher also failed to recognize the intimate relationship between language, thought, culture, and context. When this relationship is fractured by discounting or undervaluing the important role that each component plays in meaning-making, teachers end up producing antipedagogical practices that often lead to linguistic resistance, as recounted in the Dell Hymes story of a young African American girl who willfully refused to speak the standard English of her white elementary teacher even though she demonstrated ease in doing so during recess, in the absence of her teacher.

The fact that the students were able to linguistically contextualize their language through the strategy of relying on greater language production in order to render their message clearer and more explicit points to their ability to move beyond the context-bound, face-to-face communicative situation in which shared knowledge, in addition to other extralinguistic clues, facilitates meaning-making. However, my analysis of student and teacher language during the academic discourse events suggests that these events did not constitute learning situations likely to call forth students' use of linguistically contextualized language. There was little need for the students to produce language that was overtly explicit and precise, as required by the academic discourse conventions. Furthermore, the teacher failed to teach these conventions explicitly and to build on the students' existing skills for linguistically contextualizing their language—a process that possibly could have enabled her students to master both the linguistic complexity of academic discourse and the pragmatic rules that determine its proper function in different sociocultural contexts.

In an attempt to maintain cultural solidarity with her Mexican American students, the teacher created an unintentional laissez-faire teaching and learning situation, in which students were not challenged to communicate information and knowledge to imaginary distant audiences using academic discourse conventions. In fact, the teacher's overly collaborative efforts and lack of explicit instruction could be detrimental to her students' further development of academic discourse skills. Because she was so quick to assist and provide students with the correct responses, they were often not challenged to formulate the responses for themselves. In addition, because of her eagerness to always maintain a "comfort zone" by avoiding direct challenges to her students, the children did not perceive the need to treat the teacher or their peers as believable distant audiences and to linguistically contextualize their language in more conventional academic ways.

Even though the teacher was very caring and provided a supportive environment, her students were not being explicitly assisted in developing and improving their academic communicative competence. The teacher's focus on the affective dimension of teaching so as to maintain cultural solidarity with her students, even though she sacrificed her own teaching objectives, points to the inability of many teachers to understand the false dichotomy between loving one's students (particularly if they are from a subordinate minority class) and challenging them through rigorous academic work. As Paulo Freire so succinctly noted, the need to love the students and establish a more intimate cultural solidarity "should [never] reduce teaching to merely a feel-good process . . . that takes the form of paternalistic coddling." Furthermore, he explained that, in our exemplary mission as caring teachers, we cannot reconcile a nurturing posture with "a professional task that requires constant intellectual rigor and the stimulation of epistemological curiosity . . . of creativity, of scientific competence."[3]

Although the purpose of my book is not to critique the teacher's instructional approaches, I would be remiss not to point out how easy it is for many well-intentioned, hardworking, and caring teachers to fall prey to reductionistic binarisms in which caring for one's students means denying them the very academic tools they need for success. In this particular classroom, I observed a teacher who, in her attempt to love her students and be loved by them, was inadvertently failing to prepare her students for the rigors of academic learning. More important, she did not build on the students' abilities to linguistically contextualize their language by tapping their existing linguistic knowledge and communicative competence. All her good intentions led her to also become a victim of a pedagogy that miseducates.

As Paulo Freire explains, caring for one's students is insufficient to ensure effective instruction of students from subordinated cultures. Freire contends that teachers must also possess political clarity so as to be able to effectively create teaching approaches that simultaneously respect and challenge learners from diverse cultural groups in a variety of learning environments. Teachers working toward political clarity understand that they can either maintain the status quo, or they can work to transform the sociocultural reality at the classroom and school level so that the culture at this micro-level does not reflect macro-level inequalities. In the face of such formidable obstacles, they understand that, while it is important to authentically care for their students, love alone is insufficient for improving the academic opportunities and life chances of subordinated students.

Notes

Chapter One

1. The phrase *low-status linguistic-minority* refers to culturally and linguistically distinct groups that are also politically, socially, and economically subordinate in the greater society. Though individual members of these groups may not consider themselves subordinate in any manner to the English-speaking white "mainstream," they nevertheless are members of a greater collective that historically has been perceived and treated as subordinate and inferior by the dominant society.

2. Angela Carrasquillo explained that the term *Latino* is used in the United States to identify persons of Spanish-speaking origin or descent who designate themselves as Mexican American, Chicano, Puerto Rican, Cuban, or of other Hispanic origin. There are an estimated 20 million Latinos in the United States, and approximately 12.1 million (63 percent) of these individuals are of Mexican American origin. Latinos are one of the fastest-growing segments of the population in the United States. It is estimated that by the year 2000, 30 million (or 10 percent of the total U.S. population) and about 16 percent of school-aged children and persons 18 to 24 years of age will be Latino. See Carrasquillo, A. L. (1991). *Hispanic Children and Youth in the United States.* New York: Garland Publishing).

3. For a more in-depth discussion of Chicano academic underachievement, see Valencia, Richard (1991). *Chicano School Failure and Success: Research and Policy Agendas for the 1990s.* New York: Falmer Press.

4. National Commission on Secondary Education for Hispanics (1984). *"Make Something Happen": Hispanics and Urban High School Reform,* vol. 1, *Report of the National Commission on Secondary Education for Hispanics.* New York: Hispanic Policy Development Project.

5. For in-depth discussions regarding the reported relationship between academic achievement and English language proficiency over time, see: Arias, M. B. (1986). "The Context of Education for Hispanic Students: An Overview." *American Journal of Education,* 95(1): 26–57; Cummins, J. (1989). *Empowering Minority Students.* Sacramento: California Association for Bilingual Education; and Macedo, D. (1994). *Literacies of Power: What Americans Are Not Allowed to Know.* Boulder: Westview Press.

6. Arias, M. B. (1986). "The Context of Education for Hispanic Students: An Overview." *American Journal of Education,* 95(1): 26–57; Carrasquillo, A. L. (1991). *Hispanic Children and Youth in the United States.* New York: Garland Publishing.

7. Kimball, W. L. (1968). "Parent and Family Influences on Academic Achievement Among Mexican-American Students." Ph.D. diss., University of California at Los Angeles; Baral, D. (1977). *Academic Level Among Foreign-Born and Native-Born Mexican-American Students*. San Francisco: R & E Associates; and Suárez-Orozco, C., and M. Suárez-Orozco (1995). *Trans-Formations: Immigration, Family Life, and Achievement Motivation Among Latino Adolescents*. Stanford: Stanford University Press.

8. Gee, J. P. (1990). *Sociolinguistics and Literacies: Ideology in Discourses*. London: Falmer Press; Michaels, S. (1986). "Narrative Presentations: An Oral Preparation for Literacy for First Graders." In J. Cook-Gumperz (ed.), *The Social Construction of Literacy*. New York: Cambridge University Press; Michaels, S., and J. Collins (1984). "Oral Discourse Styles: Classroom Interaction and the Acquisition of Literacy." In D. Tannen (ed.), *Coherence in Spoken and Written Discourse*. Norwood, N.J.: Ablex; Collins, J., and S. Michaels (1986). "Speaking and Writing: Discourse Strategies and the Acquisition of Literacy." In J. Cook-Gumperz (ed.), *The Social Construction of Literacy*. New York: Cambridge University Press.

9. *Sharing time* refers to a narrative event common in primary elementary classrooms. During this narrative event, individual children are selected by the teacher to verbally share an object or important event with the class. The child typically stands at the front of the class facing his or her peers and orally presents on a topic or thing.

10. Michaels, S. (1986). "Narrative Presentations: An Oral Preparation for Literacy with First Graders." In J. Cook-Gumperz (ed.), *The Social Construction of Literacy*. New York: Cambridge University Press; Michaels, S., and J. Collins (1984). "Oral Discourse Styles: Classroom Interaction and the Acquisition of Literacy." In D. Tannen (ed.), *Coherence in Spoken and Written Discourse*. Norwood, N.J.: Ablex; Collins, J., and S. Michaels (1986). "Speaking and Writing: Discourse Strategies and the Acquisition of Literacy." In J. Cook-Gumperz (ed.), *The Social Construction of Literacy*. New York: Cambridge University Press.

11. Cummins, J. (1982). "The Role of Primary Language Development in Promoting Educational Success for Language Minority Students." In California State Department of Education (ed.), *Schooling and Language Minority Students: A Theoretical Framework*. Los Angeles: California State University Evaluation, Dissemination, and Assessment Center; Cummins, J. (1984). "Wanted: A Theoretical Framework for Relating Language Proficiency to Academic Achievement Among Bilingual Students." In C. Rivera (ed.), *Language Proficiency and Academic Achievement*. Avon, England: Multilingual Matters; Snow, C. F. (1987). "Beyond Conversation: Second Language Listener's Acquisition of Description and Explanation." In J. P. Lantolf and A. Labarca (eds.), *Research on Second Language Acquisition: Focus on the Classroom*. Norwood, N.J.: Ablex.

12. Macedo, D. (1994). *Literacies of Power: What Americans Are Not Allowed to Know*. Boulder: Westview Press.

13. *Academic discourses* refers to standard and more formal varieties of language; such discourses are normally called for in school situations. James Gee's comprehensive definition describes a discourse as "a socially accepted association among ways of using language, of thinking, and of acting that can be used

to identify oneself as a member of a socially meaningful group or 'social network.'". See Gee, J. G. (1991). "What Is Literacy?" In C. Mitchell and K. Weiler (eds.), *Rewriting Literacy: Culture and the Discourse of the Other.* New York: Bergin & Garvey,.

14. Pelligrini, A. D. (1984). *The Development of Oral and Written Language in Social Contexts.* Norwood, N.J.: Ablex.

15. Olson, D. T. (1977). "From Utterance to Text: The Bias of Language in Speech and Writing." *Harvard Educational Review,* 47(3): 257–281.

16. Cook-Gumperz, J., and J. J. Gumperz. (1981). "From Oral to Written Culture: The Transition to Literacy." In M. F. Whiteman (ed.), *Writing: The Nature, Development and Teaching of Written Communication,* vol. 1. New York: Cambridge University Press.

17. Donaldson, M. (1978). *Children's Minds.* London: Fantana.

18. Cummins, J. (1984). "Wanted: A Theoretical Framework for Relating Language Proficiency to Academic Achievement Among Bilingual Students." In C. Rivera (ed.), *Language Proficiency and Academic Achievement.* Avon, England: Multilingual Matters; Cummins, J. (1984). *Bilingualism and Special Education: Issues in Assessment and Pedagogy.* San Diego, Calif.: College Hill Press.

19. Simons, H. D., and S. Murphy (1986). "Spoken Language Strategies and Reading Acquisition." In J. Cook-Gumperz (ed.), *The Social Construction of Literacy.* New York: Cambridge University Press.

20. Gee, J. P. (1992). "Reading." *Journal of Urban and Cultural Studies,* 2(2): 65–77.

21. Ibid., p. 66.

22. Ibid., pp. 66–67.

23. Ibid., p. 74.

24. Ibid., p. 73.

25. Gee, J. P. (1990). *Sociolinguistics and Literacies: Ideology in Discourses.* London: Falmer Press, p. 60.

26. Michaels, S., and M. Collins (1984). "Oral Discourse Styles: Classroom Interaction and the Acquisition of Literacy." In D. Tannen (ed.), *Coherence in Spoken and Written Discourse.* Norwood, N.J.: Ablex.

27. Gee, J. P. (1990). *Sociolinguistics and Literacies: Ideology in Discourses.* London: Falmer Press; Olson, D. T. (1977). "From Utterance to Text: The Bias of Language of Speech and Writing." *Harvard Educational Review,* 47(3): 257–281.

28. Gee, J. P. (1990). *Sociolinguistics and Literacies: Ideology in Discourses.* London: Falmer Press, p. 60.

29. Rodino, A. M. (1992). "'Y . . . no puedo decir más na': The Maintenance of Native Language Skills by Working-Class Puerto Rican Children in Mainland Schools." Qualifying paper, Harvard Graduate School of Education, Cambridge, Mass., pp. 10–11.

30. McCollum, P. (1994). "Language Use in Two-Way Bilingual Programs." *Intercultural Development Research Association Newsletter,* 21(2): 1, 9–11. Shannon, S. M. (1995). "Hegemony of English: A Case Study of One Bilingual Classroom as a Site of Resistance." *Linguistics and Education,* 7(3): 175–200.

31. For an example of research showing that African American children, at a very young age, acquire a repertoire of more formal registers as part of their

communicative competence, see Anderson, Elaine S. (1990). *Speaking with Style: The Sociolinguistic Skills of Children.* New York: Routledge Press.

32. Personal communication, 1988.

33. For specific studies that examine the contextualizing strategies of African American students, see Michaels, S. (1986). "Narrative Presentations: An Oral Preparation for Literacy with First Graders." In J. Cook-Gumperz (ed.), *The Social Construction of Literacy.* New York: Cambridge University Press; Gee, J. P. (1990). *Social Linguistics and Literacies: Ideology in Discourses.* New York: Falmer Press; Michaels, S., and J. Collins (1984). "Oral Discourse Styles: Classroom Interaction and the Acquisition of Literacy." In D. Tannen (ed.), *Coherence in Spoken and Written Discourse.* Norwood, N.J.: Ablex; and Simons, H. D., and S. Murphy (1986). "Spoken Language Strategies and Reading Acquisition." In J. Cook-Gumperz (ed.), *The Social Construction of Literacy.* New York: Cambridge University Press.

34. Rodino, A. M. (1992). "'Y . . . no puedo decir más na': The Maintenance of Native Language Skills by Working-Class Puerto Rican Children in Mainland Schools." Qualifying paper, Harvard Graduate School of Education, Cambridge, Mass.; Lanauze, M., and C. E. Snow (1989). "The Relation Between First- and Second-Language Writing Skills: Evidence from Puerto Rican Elementary School Children in Bilingual Programs." *Linguistics and Education*, 1, pp. 323–339.

35. See Snow, C. E., H. Cancino, P. Gonzales, and E. Shribero (1989). "Giving Formal Definitions: An Oral Language Correlate of School Literacy." In D. Bloome (ed.), *Classrooms and Literacy.* Norwood, N.J.: Ablex; Ricard, R. J., and C. E. Snow (1990). "Language Use In and Out of Context: Evidence from Children's Picture Descriptions." *Journal of Applied Developmental Psychology*, 11(3): 251–266; Wu, H. F., J. M. De Temple, J. A. Herman, and C. E. Snow (1994). "'L'Animal qui fait oink! oink!': Bilingual Children's Oral and Written Picture Descriptions in English and French Under Varying Instructions." *Discourse Processes*, 18(2): 141–164.

36. Cummins, J. (1979). "Linguistic Interdependence and the Educational Development of Bilingual Children." *Review of Educational Research*, 49(2) 222–251; Snow, C. E. (1990). "The Development of Definitional Skill." *Journal of Child Language*, 17(3): 697–710; Lanauze, M., and C. E. Snow (1989). "The Relation Between First- and Second-Language Writing Skills: Evidence from Puerto Rican Elementary School Children in Bilingual Programs." *Linguistics and Education*, 1, pp. 323–339.

37. Ochoa, A. M. (1980). *Issues in Language Proficiency Assessment.* San Diego: Institute for Cultural Pluralism, College of Education, San Diego State University..

38. Snow, C. E., H. Cancino, P. Gonzales, and E. Shribero (1989). "Giving Formal Definitions: An Oral Language Correlate of School Literacy." In D. Bloome (ed.), *Classrooms and Literacy.* Norwood, N.J.: Ablex.

39. In the case of six of the eight target students, both parents were both Mexican American. Two of the target students (Evaristo and Oscar) came from families in which one parent was Mexican American and the other was from another Latino group. The children, however, self-identified as Mexican American.

40. Cummins, J. (1989). *Empowering Minority Students.* Sacramento: California Association for Bilingual Education.; Ogbu, J. (1991). "Immigrant and Invol-

untary Minorities in Comparative Perspective." In M. Gibson and J. Ogbu (eds.), *Minority Status and Schooling: A Comparative Study of Immigrant and Involuntary Minorities.* New York: Garland Publishing.

Chapter Two

1. Freire, P (1985). *The Politics of Education.* South Hadley, Mass.: Bergin & Garvey; Tharp, R. G., and R. Gallimore (1988). *Rousing Minds to Life: Teaching, Learning and Schooling in Social Context.* New York: Cambridge University Press; Langer, J. A. (1987). "A Sociocognitive Perspective on Literacy." In J. A. Langer (ed.), *Language, Literacy, and Culture: Issues of Society and Schooling.* Norwood, N.J.: Ablex; Vygotsky, L. (1978). *Mind and Society: The Development of Higher Psychological Processes.* Cambridge, Mass.: Harvard University Press; Vygotsky, L. (1962). *Thought and Language.* (E. Hanfmann and G. Vakar, trans.). Cambridge, Mass.: MIT Press; Gee, J. P. (1990). *Sociolinguistics and Literacies: Ideology in Discourses.* London: Falmer Press.

2. Giroux, H. (1987) "Introduction." In P. Freire and D. Macedo (eds.), *Literacy: Reading the Word and the World.* South Hadley, Mass.: Bergin & Garvey, p. XXI. Emphasis added.

3. For an in-depth discussion of this phenomenon, see Freire, P., and D. Macedo (1987). *Literacy: Reading the Word and the World.* South Hadley, Mass.: Bergin & Garvey, pp. 120–140.

4. For a more in-depth discussion of this transformation process, see L. I. Bartolomé (1994). "Beyond the Methods Fetish: Toward a Humanizing Pedagogy." *Harvard Educational Review,* 64(2): 173–194.

5. Gee, J. P. (1990). *Sociolinguistics and Literacies: Ideology in Discourses.* London: Falmer Press; Gee, J. P. (1992). "Reading." *Journal of Urban and Cultural Studies,* 2(2); Gee, J. P. (1991). "What Is Literacy?" In C. Mitchell and K. Weiler (eds.), *Rewriting Literacy: Culture and the Discourse of the Other.* New York: Bergin & Garvey.

6. Gee, J. P. (1990). *Sociolinguistics and Literacies: Ideology in Discourses.* London: Falmer Press, p. 137.

7. Ibid., p. 143.

8. Ibid.

9. For an example of this type of study, see Bloom, G. M. (1991). "The Effects of Speech Style and Skin Color on Bilingual Teaching Candidates' and Bilingual Teachers' Attitudes Toward Mexican American Pupils." Ph.D. diss., Stanford University.

10. *Political clarity* refers to the process by which individuals achieve a deepening awareness of the sociopolitical and economic realities that shape their lives and their capacity to re-create these realities at the classroom level. In addition, it refers to the process by which individuals come to better understand possible linkages between macro-level political, economic, and social variables and subordinated groups' academic performance at the micro-level classroom. Thus, it invariably requires linkage between sociocultural structures and schooling.

11. Personal communication, 1988.

12. For examples of how one teacher makes the effort to explicitly teach standard academic discourses to linguistic-minority students, see Delpit, L. (1994). *Teaching Other People's Children.* New York: New Press, pp. 40–42, "The Silenced Dialogue."

13. Giroux, H. A., and P. McLaren (1986). "Teacher Education and the Politics of Engagement: The Case for Democratic Schooling." *Harvard Educational Review,* 56(3): 213–238.

14. Gee, J. P. (1990). *Sociolinguistics and Literacies: Ideology in Discourses.* London: Falmer Press, p. 146.

15. However, it is necessary to recognize that discourses that historically have been highly valued have had the opportunity to become more developed (for example, technical concepts and vocabulary), given their use in academic and intellectual domains.

16. Heath, S. B. (1982). "What No Bedtime Story Means." *Language in Society,* 11(1): 49–76; Heath, S. B. (1982). "Questioning at Home and at School: A Comparative Study." In G. Spindler (ed.), *Doing Ethnography of Schooling: Educational Anthropology in Action.* New York: Holt, Rinehart and Winston; Heath, S. B. (1983). *Ways with Words.* New York: Cambridge University Press; Heath, S. B. (1986). "Sociocultural Contexts of Language Development." In California State Department of Education (ed.), *Beyond Language: Social and Cultural Factors in Schooling Minority Student*s. Los Angeles: California State University Evaluation, Dissemination and Assessment Center.

17. Heath, S. B. (1982). "Questioning at Home and at School: A Comparative Study. In G. Spindler (ed.), *Doing Ethnography of Schooling: Educational Anthropology in Action.* New York: Holt, Rinehart and Winston, p. 100.

18. Heath, S. B. (1983). *Ways with Words.* New York: Cambridge University Press, pp. 9–10. Emphasis added.

19. Philips, Susan U. (1972)."Participant Structures and Communication Competence: Warm Springs Children in Community and Classroom." In Courtney B. Cazden, Vera P. John, and Dell Hymes (eds.), *Functions of Language in the Classroom.* New York: Teachers College, Columbia University. Philips, S. U. (1983). *The Invisible Culture: Communication in Classroom and Community on the Warm Springs Indian Reservation.* Research on Teaching Monograph Series. New York: Longman.

20. Ibid., p. 375.

21. Au , K. H. (1979). "Using the Experience Text Relationship Method with Minority Children." *The Reading Teacher,* 32(6):677–679; Au, K. H. (1980). "Participation Structures in a Reading Lesson with Hawaiian Children: Analysis of a Culturally Appropriate Instructional Event." *Anthropology and Education Quarterly,* 11(2): 91–115; Au, K. H., and J. Mason (1983). "Cultural Congruence in Classroom Participation Structures." *Discourse Processes,* 6(4): 145–168.

22. Au, K. H., and J. Mason (1983). "Cultural Congruence in Classroom Participation Structures." *Discourse Processes,* 6(4): 148.

23. Personal communication with Ron Gallimore, 1988.

24. Villegas, A. M. (1988). "School Failure and Cultural Mismatch: Another View." *Urban Review,* 20(4): 253–265. Emphasis added.

25. Au, K. H., and J. Mason (1983). "Cultural Congruence in Classroom Participation Structures." *Discourse Processes,* 6(4): 145. Emphasis added.

26. Snow, C. E. (1987). "Beyond Conversation: Second Language Listener's Acquisition of Description and Explanation." In J. P. Lantolf and A. Labarca (eds.), *Research on Second Language Acquisition: Focus on the Classroom.* Norwood, N.J.: Ablex; Snow, C. E., H. Cancino, P. Gonzales, and E. Shribero. (1989). "Giving Formal Definitions: An Oral Language Correlate of School Literacy." In D. Bloome (ed.), *Classrooms and Literacy.* Norwood, N.J.: Ablex.

27. Gumperz, J. J., H. Keltman, and M. C. O'Connor (1984). "Cohesion in Spoken and Written Discourse: Ethnic Style and Transition to Literacy." In D. Tannen (ed.), *Coherence in Spoken and Written Discourse,* vol. 12. Norwood, N.J.: Ablex; Michaels, S., and J. Collins (1984). "Oral Discourse Styles: Classroom Interaction and the Acquisition of Literacy." In D. Tannen (ed.), *Coherence in Spoken and Written Discourse,* vol. 12. Norwood, N.J.: Ablex; Simons, H. D., and S. Murphy (1986). "Spoken Language Strategies and Reading Acquisition." In J. Cook-Gumperz (ed.), *The Social Construction of Literacy.* New York: Cambridge University Press.

28. Michaels, S., and J. Collins (1984). "Oral Discourse Styles: Classroom Interaction and the Acquisition of Literacy." In D. Tannen (ed.), *Coherence in Spoken and Written Discourse,* vol. 12. Norwood, N.J.: Ablex; Simons, H. D., and S. Murphy (1986). "Spoken Language Strategies and Reading Acquisition." In J. Cook-Gumperz (ed.), *The Social Construction of Literacy.* New York: Cambridge University Press.

29. Snow, C. E. (1987). "Beyond Conversation: Second Language Listener's Acquisition of Description and Explanation." In J. P. Lantolf and A. Labarca (eds.), *Research on Second Language Acquisition: Focus on the Classroom,* Norwood, N.J.: Ablex, p. 8.

30. Cook Gumperz, J., and J. J. Gumperz (1981). "From Oral to Written Culture: The Transition to Literacy." In M. F. Whiteman (ed.), *Writing: The Nature, Development and Teaching of Written Communication,* vol. 1. New York: Cambridge University Press, p. 93.

31. Michaels, S., and J. Collins (1984). "Oral Discourse Styles: Classroom Interaction and the Acquisition of Literacy." In D. Tannen (ed.), *Coherence in Spoken and Written Discourse.* Norwood, N.J.: Ablex.

32. The Simons and Murphy (1986) study grew out of data collected by the School-Home Ethnography Project originally conducted by Simons and Gumperz in 1980.

33. Wells, G. (1985). "Preschool Literacy-Related Activities and Success in School." In D. R. Olson, N. Torrance, and A. Hildyard (eds.), *Literacy, Language, and Learning.* Cambridge, Mass.: Cambridge University Press.

34. Snow, C. E. (1987). "Beyond Conversation: Second Language Listener's Acquisition of Description and Explanation." In J. P. Lantolf and A. Labarca (eds.), *Research on Second Language Acquisition: Focus on the Classroom,* Norwood, N.J.: Ablex; Snow, C. E., H. Cancino, P. Gonzales, and E. Shribero (1989). "Giving Formal Definitions: An Oral Language Correlate of School Literacy." In D. Bloome (ed.), *Classrooms and Literacy.* Norwood, N.J.: Ablex.

35. Velasco, P. (1989). "The Relationship of Oral Decontextualized Language and Reading Comprehension in Bilingual Children." Ph.D. diss., Harvard Graduate School of Education, Cambridge, Mass.; Rodino, A. M. (1992). "'Y . . . no puedo decir más na': The Maintenance of Native Language Skills by Working-

Class Puerto Rican Children in Mainland Schools." Qualifying paper, Harvard Graduate School of Education, Cambridge, Mass.

36. Wells, G. (1981). *Learning Through Interaction*. London: Cambridge University Press; Wells, G. (1982). "Influences of the Home on Language Development." In A. Davies (ed.), *Language and Learning in Home and School*. London: Heinemann ; Snow, C. E. (1987). "Beyond Conversation: Second Language Listener's Acquisition of Description and Explanation." In J. P. Lantolf and A. Labarca (eds.), *Research on Second Language Acquisition: Focus on the Classroom*. Norwood, N.J.: Ablex; Snow, C. E., H. Cancino, P. Gonzales, and E. Shribero (1989). "Giving Formal Definitions: An Oral Language Correlate of School Literacy." In D. Bloome (ed.), *Classrooms and Literacy*. Norwood, N.J.: Ablex.; Velasco, P. (1989). "The Relationship of Oral Decontextualized Language and Reading Comprehension in Bilingual Children." Ph.D. diss., Harvard Graduate School of Education, Cambridge, Mass.; Rodino, A. M. (1992). "'Y . . . no puedo decir más na': The Maintenance of Native Language Skills by Working-Class Puerto Rican Children in Mainland Schools." Qualifying paper, Harvard Graduate School of Education, Cambridge, Mass.

37. Gee, J. P. (1990). *Sociolinguistics and Literacies: Ideology in Discourses*. London: Falmer Press, p. XVII.

38. Rodino, A. M. (1992). "'Y . . . no puedo decir más na': The Maintenance of Native Language Skills by Working-Class Puerto Rican Children in Mainland Schools." Qualifying paper, Harvard Graduate School of Education, Cambridge, Mass.

39. Gee, J. P. (1990). *Sociolinguistics and Literacies: Ideology in Discourses*. London: Falmer Press, p. 149.

40. Freire, P. (1993). *A Pedagogy of the City*. New York: Continuum Press, p. 17.

41. Gee, J. P. (1990). *Sociolinguistics and Literacies: Ideology in Discourses*. London: Falmer Press, p. 159.

Chapter Three

1. I use pseudonyms to protect the identities of the participants and sites involved..

2. James Crawford described "transitional bilingual education" as education for English-language learners that allows for a portion of the instructional program to be conducted in the students' native language to help them keep up in school subjects while they study English in programs especially designed for them. The goal is to prepare English-language learners to eventually enter a mainstream English-only classroom. "Maintenance bilingual programs" attempt to maintain and further develop the English-language learners' native language while they acquire English as a second language. For additional information, refer to Crawford, J. (1991). *Bilingual Education: History, Politics, Theory, and Practice*, 2d ed. Los Angeles: Bilingual Educational Services.

3. Bilingual education expert James Cummins has maintained that second language acquisition occurs at two general levels. He pointed out that educators must distinguish between basic conversational skills and more cognitively demanding academic language abilities. He utilized the term *BICs*, or basic interpersonal communication skills, to refer to basic conversational abilities and the term

CALPs, or cognitive academic language proficiency, to refer to both "reading and writing abilities and to content areas where students are required to use their language abilities for learning" and not simply communicating. Cummins explained that it takes the second language learner approximately two years to acquire basic interpersonal communication skills and anywhere from five to seven years to acquire cognitive academic language proficiency. For a more in-depth discussion of these two types of language proficiency please see Cummins, J. (1989). *Empowering Minority Students.* Sacramento: California Association for Bilingual Education, pp. 21–34.

4. California State Department of Education Bilingual Education Office (1987). "Districts Ranked by Enrollment of Limited English Proficient Students." Listing compiled by the California State Department of Education, Sacramento, Calif.

5. Chall, J. S. (1983). *Stages of Reading Development.* New York: McGraw-Hill; Snow, C. E. (1987). "Beyond Conversation: Second Language Listener's Acquisition of Description and Explanation." In J. P. Lantolf and A. Labarca (eds.), *Research on Second Language Acquisition: Focus on the Classroom,* Norwood, N.J.: Ablex; Snow, C. E., H. Cancino, P. Gonzales, and E. Shribero (1987). *Second Language Learners' Formal Definitions: An Oral Language Correlate of School Literacy.* Los Angeles: University of California at Los Angeles Center for Language Education and Research.

6. Ochoa, A. M. (1980). *Issues in Language Proficiency Assessment.* San Diego: Institute for Cultural Pluralism, College of Education, San Diego State University.

7. There is currently disagreement regarding whether students who have recently immigrated achieve academically at higher rates than their U.S.-born peers. I purposely matched students so that the only discernible difference was in terms of standardized tests scores. All children received their schooling in U.S. schools only and were identified by their schools as English proficient; thus, there were no performance differences due to lack of English proficiency or foreign academic preparation.

For a historical view of this debate, see Baral, D. P. (1977). *Academic Level Among Foreign-Born and Native-Born Mexican American Students.* San Francisco: R & E Associates; Dulay, H. C., and M. K. Burt (1980). "The Relative Proficiency of Limited English Proficient Students." *Journal of the National Association of Bilingual Education,* 4(3): 1–23; McCarthy, K., and R. Burciaga-Váldez (1985). *Current and Future Effects of Mexican Immigration in California* Monograph no. R.–3365/1-CR. Santa Monica, Calif.: Rand Corporation; Suárez-Orozco, C., and M. Suárez-Orozco (1995*). Trans-Formations: Immigration, Family Life, and Achievement Motivation Among Latino Adolescents.* Stanford: Stanford University Press; Ogbu, J. U. (1978). *Minority Education and Caste.* New York: Academic Press.

Chapter Four

1. Cummins, J. (1989). *Empowering Minority Students.* Sacramento: California Association for Bilingual Education; Ogbu, J. (1991). "Immigrant and Involuntary Minorities in Comparative Perspective." In M. Gibson and J. Ogbu (eds.), *Minority Status and Schooling: A Comparative Study of Immigrant and Involuntary Minorities.* New York: Garland Publishing.

2. Dickenson, D. K., and C. E. Snow (1987). "Interrelationships Among Pre-Reading and Oral Language Skills in Kindergartners from Two Social Classes." *Early Childhood Research Quarterly*, 2(1):1–25.

3. Snow, C. E. (1987). "Beyond Conversation: Second Language Listener's Acquisition of Description and Explanation." In J. P. Lantolf and A. Labarca (eds.), *Research on Second Language Acquisition: Focus on the Classroom*. Norwood, N.J.: Ablex.

4. Mehan, H. (1979). *Learning Lessons*. Cambridge, Mass.: Harvard University Press; Mehan, H. (1979). "'What Time Is It, Denise?' Asking Known Information Questions in Classroom Discourse." *Theory into Practice*, 18(4):285–294.

5. Snow, C. E. (1987). "Beyond Conversation: Second Language Listener's Acquisition of Description and Explanation." In J. P. Lantolf and A. Labarca (eds.), *Research on Second Language Acquisition: Focus on the Classroom*. Norwood, N.J.: Ablex; Dickenson, D. K., and C. E. Snow (1987). "Interrelationships Among Pre-Reading and Oral Language Skills in Kindergartners from Two Social Classes." *Early Childhood Research Quarterly*, 2(1):1–25.

6. Andersen, E. S. (1990). *Speaking with Style: Skills of Children*. New York: Routledge; Cazden, C. (1986). "Classroom Discourse." In M. C. Wittrock (ed.), *Handbook of Research on Teaching*, 3d ed. New York: Macmillan, pp. 432–463; Cazden, C. (1988). *Classroom Discourse: The Language of Teaching and Learning*. Portsmouth, N.H.: Heinemann; Mehan, H. (1979). *Learning Lessons*. Cambridge, Mass.: Harvard University Press; Mehan, H. (1979). "'What Time Is It, Denise?' Asking Known Information Questions in Classroom Discourse." *Theory into Practice*, 18(4):285–294.

7. Langer, J. A., L. I. Bartolomé, O. A. Vasquez, and T. Lucas (1990). "Meaning Construction in School Literacy Tasks: A Study of Bilingual Students." *American Educational Research Journal*, 27(3): 427–471; Snow, C. E. (1987). "Beyond Conversation: Second Language Listener's Acquisition of Description and Explanation." In J. P. Lantolf and A. Labarca (eds.), *Research on Second Language Acquisition: Focus on the Classroom*. Norwood, N.J.: Ablex.

8. Snow, C. E. (1987). "Beyond Conversation: Second Language Listener's Acquisition of Description and Explanation." In J. P. Lantolf and A. Labarca (eds.), *Research on Second Language Acquisition: Focus on the Classroom*. Norwood, N.J.: Ablex.

9. Perrera, K. (1984). *Children's Writing and Reading: Analyzing Classroom Language*. New York: Basil Blackwell.

10. Edelsky, C. (1989). "Bilingual Children's Writing: Fact and Fiction." In D. M. Johnson and D. H. Roen (eds.), *Richness in Writing: Empowering ESL Students*. White Plains, N.Y.: Longman, p. 167.

11. Ibid.

12. Roen, D. H.(1989). "Developing Effective Assignments for Second Language Writers." In D. M. Johnson and D. H. Roen (eds.), *Richness in Writing: Empowering ESL Students*. White Plains, N.Y.: Longman.

13. Cazden, C. (1986). "Classroom Discourse." In M. C. Wittrock (ed.), *Handbook of Research on Teaching*, 3d ed. New York: Macmillan, pp. 432–463; Cazden, C. (1988). *Classroom Discourse: The Language of Teaching and Learning*. Portsmouth, N.H.: Heinemann; Mehan, H. (1979). *Learning Lessons*. Cambridge, Mass.: Harvard University Press; Mehan, H. (1979). "'What Time Is It, Denise?' Ask-

ing Known Information Questions in Classroom Discourse." *Theory into Practice*, 18(4):285–294.

Chapter Five

1. Snow, C. E. (1987). "Beyond Conversation: Second Language Listener's Acquisition of Description and Explanation." In J. P. Lantolf and A. Labarca (eds.), *Research on Second Language Acquisition: Focus on the Classroom*, Norwood, N.J.: Ablex; Snow, C. E., H. Cancino, P. Gonzales, and E. Shribero (1989). "Giving Formal Definitions: An Oral Language Correlate of School Literacy." In D. Bloome (ed.), *Classrooms and Literacy*. Norwood, N.J.: Ablex.

2. Davidson, R. G., S. B. Kline, and C. E. Snow (1986). "Definitions and Definite Noun Phrases: Indicators of Children's Decontextualized Language Skills." *Journal of Research in Childhood Education*, 1(1):42.

3. Description of tasks are modified from Davidson, R. G., S. B. Kline, and C. E. Snow (1986). "Definitions and Definite Noun Phrases: Indicators of Children's Decontextualized Language Skills." *Journal of Research in Childhood Education*, 1(1):42.

4. A *clarificatory marker* modifies a noun but is not an adjective. A clarificatory marker can be a clause (the boy you met *last night* is my brother), a prepositional phrase (the girl *on your left* is my sister), a participial phrase (the dog running *down the street* has rabies), or an appositive (our new car, *an '87* BMW, was towed this morning). A *locative* gives a relatively specific place, direction, goal, or source—e.g., John is *behind* the tree; he went *to the beach*; she sent the letter *to me*; she picked up shells *from the beach*. Coding manual developed by C. E. Snow (1986), Harvard Graduate School of Education, Cambridge, Mass.

5. Loban, W. (1976). *Language Development: Kindergarten Through Grade Twelve*. NCTE Research Report no. 18. Urbana, Ill.: National Council of Teachers of English.

6. "[The] logic for distinguishing linguistically contextualized from contextualized responses derives from the syntax of formal noun definitions in English and French which requires a statement of class membership followed by a specification of the proper subset of the class (for example, 'a car is a motorized passenger vehicle which travels on four wheels')." For additional information, see Davidson, R. G., S. B. Kline, and C. E. Snow (1986). "Definitions and Definite Noun Phrases: Indicators of Children's Decontextualized Language Skills." *Journal of Research in Childhood Education*, 1(1):41.

Chapter Six

1. Freire, P. (1997). *Pedagogy of the Heart*. New York: Continuum Publishing Group, p. 43.

2. Jacob is cited in Freire, P. (1997). *Teachers as Cultural Workers: Letters to Those Who Dare Teach*. Boulder, Westview Press, p. 69.

3. Freire, P. (1998). *Teachers as Cultural Workers: Letters to Those Who Dare Teach*. Boulder: Westview Press, p. 4.

Index

Academic discourse
  access to, *xii, xiii*, 2, 3, 4, 7, 26, 110.
    See also Mentoring
  in classroom study, 63–66
  defined, 2, 3, 4, 124(n13)
  and values, 5–6
  See also Discourse, dominant;
    Linguistically contextualized
    language; Secondary discourse
Academic proficiency. *See* English
  language, proficiency in; Student
  competency
Adjective use, 41. *See also* Clarificatory
  markers
African American students, 2, 11–12,
  13, 29–30, 31–32, 37, 38, 41
Anglo students. *See* White American
  students
Apprenticeship, 21, 27, 42, 43–45. *See*
  also Mentoring; Modeling
Au, Katheryn Hu-Pei, 33, 34, 35
Audience, as interlocutor, 8, 10
  in classroom study, 66–67, 73, 78, 79
  in language tasks, 65, 88, 89, 90, 94,
    95, 96–97, 98–99, 100, 101,
    102–106, 110, 116, 118
  peer role as, 76–78
  teacher role as, 68, 69, 72, 73, 74–76

Basic interpersonal communication
  skills (BICs), 48, 130(n3)
BICs. *See* Basic interpersonal
  communication skills
Bilingual education, 3

classroom study in, 47–51, 63–85.
  See also Picture description tasks;
  Word definition tasks
  maintenance, 48, 49, 50, 130(n2)
  transitional, 48, 130(n2)
  See also English language; Spanish
    language
Boggs, Stephen T., 33
Book language, 39–40. *See also*
  Linguistically contextualized
  language

CALPs. *See* Cognitive academic
  language proficiency
Cárdenas, José, 12
Clarificatory markers, 93, 94, 95, 102,
  103, 133(n4)
Class, 14, 65, 85
Classroom performance, studies of,
  32–36, 47–51
  of oral presentations, 74–78
  student profiles and activities in,
    51–59, 82
  teacher objectives and practices in,
    43, 64, 65, 67–68, 72, 73–76, 78,
    79–85, 121
  teacher profile in, 47–49, 119
  in word definitions, 67–72
  in writing activities, 78–84
  See also Audience; Bilingual
    education; Explicitness;
    Language performance tasks;
    Teacher-student interaction
Code-switching, 102, 103, 104, 118

Picture description tasks, 41, 88–90,
116
language production in, 90–93
narrative strategies in, 93–95
student examples of, 95–106
Political clarity, 24, 127(n10)
Political dimensions, of discourse
teaching, 19, 20, 21, 24, 27. //See
also Discourse, dominant; Power
relations; Valuation
Powerful discourses, 26
Power relations
sociocultural, *xii*, 17, 18, 19, 20, 21,
27, 35
teacher-student, 34–36, 83
See also Mentoring; Socialization;
Student resistance; Valuation
Primary discourse, 22–23, 26–27, 120
middle-class, 27, 42
Privilege, 42
Pronoun use, 38–39, 96, 99
Psychological effects, of discourse
teaching, 11, 12, 24. See also
Valuation
Puerto Rican American students, 41

Racial subjugation, 29–32
Reading achievement, 29, 30, 31,
39–40, 41
Rodino, Ana María, 10, 41, 43

School-Home Ethnography Project,
38–39
Secondary discourse, 22–23, 24–26,
42–43
critical appropriation of, 26–27
Second language learning, 2, 14, 15, 64
Shared knowledge, *ix*, 2, 9, 96, 98, 99,
106, 107, 113, 115, 116, 120
Sharing (show and tell) time, 8, 37–38,
124(n9)
Simons, Herbert, 38–39
Snow, Catherine, 14, 21, 40, 67, 88
Socialization, *xv*, 8, 23, 24–25, 117,
119. See also Cultural
incongruence; Power relations;
Valuation

Spanish language
loss of, 41
picture description tasks in, 88, 89,
92, 93, 94–95, 101–106
word definition tasks in, 108–115
Standard discourse. See Academic
discourse
Storytelling, 40, 48
Student competency, 12, 17, 23, 43, 72,
84
Student resistance, 11, 12, 64, 84, 120.
See also Valuation
Subjugation, racial, 29–32

Talk story, 33–34
Teacher-student interaction, 23, 26
in oral presentations, 72–78
in word definition exercises, 67–72
in writing activities, 78–84
See also Classroom performance;
Cultural incongruence; Cultural
solidarity; Mentoring; Political
clarity; Power relations; Student
resistance
Topic organization, 8, 37–38
T-unit production, 81–82, 88, 90–93,
119

Upper class, 14, 41

Valuation, of discourses, *xv*, 4, 6, 8–9,
10–11, 12, 19–20, 22, 23, 27, 117,
128(n5). See also Power relations
Velasco, Patricia, 41
Verbal participation, 33–34. See also
Oral participation
Villegas, Ana María, 35
Vocabulary exercises. See Word
definition tasks
Vygotsky, Lev, 18

Watson-Gegeo, Karen, 33
Wechsler Intelligence Scale for
Children (WISC-R), 40, 106
Wells, Gordon, 39–40, 41
White American students, 29, 31,
37–38, 41

WISC-R. *See* Wechsler Intelligence
  Scale for Children
Word definition tasks
  in classroom exercise, 64, 66, 67–72
  formal/informal, 40, 106–107,
    108–109, 110, 112–116, 133(n6)
  functional statements in, 113–114,
    115(table)
  relative clause and superordinate
    use in, 110–112

Working-class students, 29–32, 37–38,
    41, 42, 51, 117, 131(n7). *See also*
    Linguistic-minority students
Writing activities
  authentic and simulated, 83
  on picture description tasks,
    compared to oral, 88–106
  solitary, 78–83, 84
  on word definitions, 64, 67